ROSENCRANTZ AND GUILDENSTERN ARE DEAD:
THE FILM

also by Tom Stoppard

ROSENCRANTZ AND GUILDENSTERN ARE DEAD
THE REAL INSPECTOR HOUND
ENTER A FREE MAN
AFTER MAGRITTE
JUMPERS
TRAVESTIES
DIRTY LINEN and NEW-FOUND-LAND
EVERY GOOD BOY DESERVES FAVOUR
and PROFESSIONAL FOUL
NIGHT AND DAY
DOGG'S HAMLET, CAHOOT'S MACBETH
DALLIANCE and UNDISCOVERED COUNTRY
(*adapted from Arthur Schnitzler's* Das Weite Land)
ON THE RAZZLE
(*adapted from Johann Nestroy's* Einen Jux will er sich machen)
THE REAL THING
THE DOG IT WAS THAT DIED AND OTHER PLAYS
SQUARING THE CIRCLE with
EVERY GOOD BOY DESERVES FAVOUR
and PROFESSIONAL FOUL
FOUR PLAYS FOR RADIO:
ARTIST DESCENDING A STAIRCASE,
WHERE ARE THEY NOW?
IF YOU'RE GLAD I'LL BE FRANK
and ALBERT'S BRIDGE
ROUGH CROSSING
(*adapted from Ferenc Molnár's* Play at the Castle)
HAPGOOD

and a novel
LORD MALQUIST AND MR MOON

Rosencrantz and Guildenstern are Dead
The Film

TOM STOPPARD

faber and faber
LONDON · BOSTON

First published in 1991
by Faber and Faber Limited
3 Queen Square London WCIN 3AU

Phototypeset by Wilmaset Birkenhead Wirral
Printed in England by Clays Ltd, St Ives Plc

Stills courtesy of Brandenberg International Ltd

A CIP record for this book is available from the British Library

ISBN 0-571-15246-5

Rosencrantz and Guildenstern are Dead: the Film opened in London in spring 1991. The cast was as follows:

ROSENCRANTZ	Gary Oldman
GUILDENSTERN	Tim Roth
THE PLAYER	Richard Dreyfuss
TRAGEDIANS	Livio Badurina
	Tomislav Maretic
	Mare Mlacnik
	Srdjan Soric
	Mladen Vasary
	Zeljko Vukmirica
	Branko Zavrsan
OPHELIA	Joanna Roth
HAMLET	Iain Glen
CLAUDIUS	Donald Sumpter
GERTRUDE	Joanna Miles
OSRIC	Ljubo Zecevic
POLONIUS	Ian Richardson
LAERTES	Sven Medvesck
HORATIO	Vili Matula
AMBASSADOR FROM ENGLAND	John Burgess
Director	Tom Stoppard
Producers	Michael Brandman
	Emanuel Azenberg
Director of Photography	Peter Biziou

EXT. QUARRY, DAY

The white screen takes on a texture and becomes grey/white stone.

From a fold in the cliff-face, two horsemen ride into view. The horses are on a ledge cut into the cliff-face. At this distance, the figures of the two horsemen are small.

EXT. QUARRY, CONTINUATION

Now we are close. ROSENCRANTZ *and* GUILDENSTERN *are cloaked and hatted against the cold. Their faces and eyes are alive. They look around as their mounts crunch their way along the track.*

The two men look like cowboys in Indian country.

GUILDENSTERN, *leading the way, reins in his horse from a walk to a stop.* ROSENCRANTZ *comes up abreast.* ROSENCRANTZ *decides to speak. But he dries on the first word, which might have been the other man's name.*

ROSENCRANTZ: Erm . . .

> (GUILDENSTERN, *preoccupied, nudges his horse forward again, and the opportunity has passed.*)

EXT. QUARRY TRACK, DAY

Something small is catching the light. Four hoofs go by. Then four more hoofs. The second lot of hoofs come back round to . . . what turns out to be a coin.

ROSENCRANTZ's *boots thump down on to the ground next to the coin.*

Now ROSENCRANTZ *is picking up the coin.*

ROSENCRANTZ

Rubs the coin on his sleeve.

He is standing by his horse.

GUILDENSTERN *has reined in his horse.*

GUILDENSTERN

Looks out into the distance.

ROSENCRANTZ
Gives the coin a little experimental flip. He catches it. We see that it lies heads up on his hand.
ROSENCRANTZ: Heads.
   (*He does this several times.*)

GUILDENSTERN
Continues to stare into the distance. He isn't listening to what we can hear. What we can hear is the small sound of ROSENCRANTZ *spinning the coin, slapping it on to the back of his hand and announcing it as* . . .
ROSENCRANTZ: Heads!
   (*Now the coin starts entering* GUILDENSTERN's *frame. It enters through the bottom of the frame and drops out of the bottom of the frame* . . . *to be announced as* . . .)
   Heads!
   (*This happens several times, until it gets through to* GUILDENSTERN *that there is something funny going on. His eyes change focus. He looks down, frowns* . . .
       The coin enters the frame again, and this time GUILDENSTERN *reaches out and intercepts it in mid-air. He looks at it.*
       GUILDENSTERN *checks the other side of the coin, and spins the coin to* ROSENCRANTZ, *casually.* ROSENCRANTZ *catches it and announces it as* . . .)
   Heads.
   (GUILDENSTERN *gives him a look.*
       ROSENCRANTZ *puts the coin in his purse, quite unaffected by the run of 'heads'.*
       GUILDENSTERN *takes a coin from a purse (pouch) hanging on his belt. He spins it, catches it.*)
   Bet? Heads I win.
   (GUILDENSTERN *nods. He turns the coin over on to his wrist and reveals it, for himself. He tosses it to* ROSENCRANTZ, *who catches it, turns it over on to his wrist but keeps it covered.*)
   Again?
   (GUILDENSTERN *nods.*
       ROSENCRANTZ *looks at the coin.*)
   Heads.

(ROSENCRANTZ *puts the coin into his own purse.*)
Again?
(GUILDENSTERN *puts his hand into his pouch for another coin.*)

EXT. TOP OF QUARRY, DAY
Now we can see sky, but ROSENCRANTZ *and* GUILDENSTERN *on their horses occupy most of the frame.*

GUILDENSTERN *leads.* ROSENCRANTZ *is still flipping a coin, the same coin each time, modestly flipped, caught, turned over . . . and announced as . . .*
ROSENCRANTZ: Heads! . . . Heads! . . . Heads! . . . And heads
    it is! . . .
    (*But then he fails to catch the coin, it bounces out of his hand
    and falls . . .*)

THE CLIFF
The camera follows the coin down the side of the cliff . . . the shot narrowing down until we are close to the face of the cliff . . . and until we see the coin bounce into frame, and we stay with the coin until it stops rolling and bouncing and falling and falls close enough for us to see that it is heads.

EXT. IN THE TREES, DAY
ROSENCRANTZ *and* GUILDENSTERN *have made a camp.*

We see the smoking fire, then the two horses, hobbled. Over this, we hear the metallic spin of the coin, the slap of a hand, and ROSENCRANTZ *muttering 'heads'.*

Now we see what is happening. GUILDENSTERN *is doing the spinning,* ROSENCRANTZ *is catching the coin. He announces each coin as heads and adds it to . . .*

About seventy coins stacked up like poker chips.
GUILDENSTERN: (*Flipping a coin to* ROSENCRANTZ) A weaker
    man might be moved to re-examine his faith, if in nothing
    else at least in the law of probability.
ROSENCRANTZ: Heads.
GUILDENSTERN: Consider. One – probability is a factor which
    operates within natural forces. Two – probability is not
    operating as a factor. Three – we are now held within un-,
    sub- or super-natural forces. Discuss!

3

ROSENCRANTZ: (*Stunned*) What?

GUILDENSTERN: Look at it this way. If six monkeys . . . if six monkeys . . .
(*He takes out another coin.*)
The law of averages, if I have got this right, means that if six monkeys were thrown up in the air for long enough they would land on their tails . . . (*He flips the coin*) . . . about as often as they would land on their –

ROSENCRANTZ: Heads.
(*He adds the coin to his pile.*) Getting a bit of a bore, isn't it?

GUILDENSTERN: A bore?

ROSENCRANTZ: Well . . .

GUILDENSTERN: What about the suspense?

ROSENCRANTZ: What suspense?

GUILDENSTERN: It must be the law of diminishing returns.
(GUILDENSTERN *stands up suddenly, taking out one of his last coins.*)
I feel the spell about to be broken!
(*He spins the coin.*)

THE COIN
Gets special treatment – slow motion, music . . .
We see ROSENCRANTZ *and* GUILDENSTERN *looking upwards towards the coin's zenith.*
GUILDENSTERN *catches the coin.*

GUILDENSTERN: Well, it was an even chance.
(GUILDENSTERN *throws the coin to* ROSENCRANTZ.
ROSENCRANTZ *picks up the coin.*)

ROSENCRANTZ: Seventy-eight in a row. A new record, I imagine.

GUILDENSTERN: A new record?

ROSENCRANTZ: Well . . .

GUILDENSTERN: No questions? Not a flicker of doubt?

ROSENCRANTZ: I could be wrong.

GUILDENSTERN: No *fear*?

ROSENCRANTZ: Fear?

GUILDENSTERN: *Fear*!
(*So saying he flings another coin at* ROSENCRANTZ.
ROSENCRANTZ *looks at it.*)

ROSENCRANTZ: (*Timidly*) Seventy-nine.

EXT. THE CAMPSITE, LATER

Time to eat.

They have been cooking.

ROSENCRANTZ *is passing the time by spinning the same coin again and again, keeping the score in a mutter.*

GUILDENSTERN: I think I have it. Time has stopped dead, and the single experience of one coin being spun once has been repeated . . .

ROSENCRANTZ: A hundred and fifty-six . . .

GUILDENSTERN: . . . a hundred and fifty-six times. On the whole, doubtful. (*A new idea:*) Or, a spectacular vindication of the principle that each individual coin spun individually is as likely to come down heads as tails and therefore should cause no surprise each individual time it does.

ROSENCRANTZ: Heads . . .

(ROSENCRANTZ *abandons the coin-spinning.*)

I've never known anything like it.

(GUILDENSTERN *starts to eat, biting into the tomato and the onion alternately, then into the bread, picking up meat in his fingers. A messy business.*)

GUILDENSTERN: He has never known anything like it. But he has never known anything to write home about. *Therefore –* it's nothing to write home about.

(ROSENCRANTZ *is placidly dealing with his food, but very differently. He has taken out a knife and is slicing the tomato and the onion.*)

What's the first thing you remember?

ROSENCRANTZ: Oh, let's see . . . the first thing that comes into my head, you mean?

GUILDENSTERN: No – the first thing you remember.

ROSENCRANTZ: Ah. (*He thinks deeply.*) No, it's no good, it's gone. It was a long time ago.

GUILDENSTERN: You don't get my meaning. What is the first thing *after* all the things you've forgotten?

ROSENCRANTZ: (*Now he gets it.*) Oh, I see. (*He thinks deeply.*) I've forgotten the question.

(*Now* ROSENCRANTZ *is slicing through the middle of his hunk of bread.*)

GUILDENSTERN: Are you happy?

ROSENCRANTZ: What?

GUILDENSTERN: Content? At ease?

ROSENCRANTZ: I suppose so.

GUILDENSTERN: What are you going to do now?

ROSENCRANTZ: I don't know. What do you want to do?

> (ROSENCRANTZ's *interest and concentration are on preparing his food*.)
> Look . . .
> (*He has invented the hamburger. He is quite pleased with himself.*
>> GUILDENSTERN *looks at the hamburger. But the march of civilization makes no impression on him.*)

GUILDENSTERN: What about it?

ROSENCRANTZ: Well . . .

GUILDENSTERN: (*Impatiently*) We have been spinning coins together since I don't know when and in all that time, if it is all that time, one hundred and fifty-seven coins spun consecutively have come down heads one hundred and fifty-seven consecutive times, and all you can do is play with your food.

> (*But then he gets a flash of something.*) There was a messenger!

INSERT: SHUTTERS

Wooden shutters, seen from inside a room, are being banged and shaken. A voice outside is shouting their names – 'Rosencrantz . . . Guildenstern!'

THE CAMPSITE

GUILDENSTERN: We were sent for.

EXT. THE WOODS

They are on horseback.

ROSENCRANTZ: Another curious scientific phenomenon is the fact that the fingernails grow after death, as does the beard.

GUILDENSTERN: What?

ROSENCRANTZ: Beard!

GUILDENSTERN: But you're not dead.

ROSENCRANTZ: I didn't say *it only started* to grow after death!

6

(*Pause.*) The fingernails also grow before birth. Though *not* the beard.

GUILDENSTERN: *What?*

ROSENCRANTZ: (*Pause.*) *Beard!* What's the matter with you? The toenails on the other hand never grow at all.

GUILDENSTERN: The toenails on the other *foot* never grow at all.

ROSENCRANTZ: No . . .

GUILDENSTERN: Do you remember the first thing that happened *today?*

ROSENCRANTZ: I woke up, I suppose. Oh – I've got it now – that man, he woke us up –

GUILDENSTERN: A messenger.

ROSENCRANTZ: That's it – pale sky before dawn, a man standing in his saddle to bang on the shutters –
shouts – what's all the row about!? Clear off! – but then he called our names. You remember that – this man woke us up.

GUILDENSTERN: Yes.

ROSENCRANTZ: We were sent for.

GUILDENSTERN: Yes.

ROSENCRANTZ: That's why we're here. (*He looks around.*) Travelling. It was urgent – a matter of extreme urgency, a royal summons, his very words – official business and no questions asked – up we get and off at the gallop, fearful lest we come too late!

GUILDENSTERN: Too late for what?

ROSENCRANTZ: How do I know? We haven't got there yet.
(GUILDENSTERN *hears something. He tilts his head, listening.*
ROSENCRANTZ *hears something. He tilts his head, listening.*
They stand listening. Now we hear it. A distant rhythmic iron clank, faint.)
I say –

EXT. THE WOODS, EVENING

THE CART
We start close on source of the noise – an iron pan hanging from the back of the cart is swinging and bumping against another iron pan.
The cart is approaching, pulled by two horses . . .

CART AND PLAYERS
There are seven TRAGEDIANS *walking with the cart.*

EXT. THE WOODS
ROSENCRANTZ *and* GUILDENSTERN *wait on their horses until the cart gets level with them.*
PLAYER: Halt!
    (*Their heads jerk upward.*
       The PLAYER *is riding on top of the box, in the act of lumbering to his feet among the bundles and boxes where he had been reclining. He bangs the roof of the cart with a stout stick.*)

THE PLAYER
Greeting them, a vagabond king stretching out his arms.
PLAYER: An audience!

THE TROUPE
Looking up, seeing ROSENCRANTZ *and* GUILDENSTERN, *desperate and dangerous-looking men, the lot of them.*

ROSENCRANTZ AND GUILDENSTERN
Recoiling.
PLAYER: Don't move!
    (*He kicks a wicker basket off the roof.*
       ROSENCRANTZ *and* GUILDENSTERN *glance at each other, looking amazed at* –)

CART AND PLAYERS
Galvanic activity. Boxes and bundles falling off the roof, the PLAYERS *ransacking them for hats, cloaks, all kinds of costumes, Alfred pitching in, ramming a woman's wig on to his head* –

PLAYER
Kicking away linchpins at the top.
   The entire side wall of the cart hinging down to make an apron stage attached to the exposed interior of the cart –
   Which is full of props (weapons, torches, musical instruments, stuffed animals, etc.) –
   Which even now are being thrown out of the back door of the cart to clear the acting space, while –

The trestles are being put in place to hold up the apron stage, which –

Turns out to be doubled on itself, hinged, and is now unfolded to double its floor space in one direction, and again the other way to double the floor space sideways too.

ROSENCRANTZ AND GUILDENSTERN
Watching, stunned.

THE PLAYER
Is on the roof, lifting a trap door.

ALFRED
Is painting his face in a mirror.

A 'Lucifer' match being struck on one of the iron wheels.

A tragedian (juggler) puts the match to a bundle of three torches he holds in his hand.

THE 'INTERIOR' OF THE STAGE
Which now has a wooden stairway like a ship's companionway, leading down from the trap door in the roof . . . down which the
PLAYER *is descending, approaching and greeting –*

ROSENCRANTZ *and* GUILDENSTERN, *thoroughly intimidated.*
PLAYER: Perfect! A lucky thing we came along!
ROSENCRANTZ: For us?
PLAYER: Also for you. For some it is performance, for others patronage, they are two sides of the same coin – or being as there are so many of us the same side of two coins. Well met, in fact, and just in time.
ROSENCRANTZ: Why's that?
PLAYER: Why, we grow rusty and you catch us at the very point of decadence – by this time tomorrow we might have forgotten everything we ever knew. We'd be back where we started, improvising.
ROSENCRANTZ: Tumblers, are you?
PLAYER: We can give you a tumble, if that's your taste, and times being what they are. Otherwise, for a jingle of coin we can do you a selection of gory romances, pirated from the Italian – and it doesn't take much to make a jingle – even a single coin has music in it, should it be gold. (*He doffs his hat with a flourish and bows.*) Tragedians, at your command.

9

(A tatty red velvet curtain drops to divide the interior stage from the forestage . . . on which the troupe of TRAGEDIANS *disposed, all gorgeously and gallantly dressed; Alfred, pretty as a girl, in a white gown, curtsying as all the others flourish and bow –*

Lit by perhaps half-a-dozen flaming torches stuck into hoops on the edge of the stage.

All very impressive.)

ROSENCRANTZ: My name is Guildenstern, and this is Rosencrantz.

(GUILDENSTERN *shakes his head.*)

I'm sorry – *his* name's Guildenstern, and *I'm* Rosencrantz.

PLAYER: We've played to bigger, but quality counts for something.

GUILDENSTERN: Tragedians? What exactly . . . ?

PLAYER: Tragedy, sir. Deaths and disclosures, universal and particular, dénouements both unexpected and inexorable, transvestite melodrama on all levels including the suggestive. We transport you into a world of intrigue and illusion –

THE TRAGEDIANS
Deftly illustrate, and loose pages of manuscript flutter from an open box, caught by the wind . . .

PLAYER: . . . clowns, if you like, murders – we can do you ghosts and battles, on the skirmish level, heroes, villains, tormented lovers – set pieces in the poetic vein – we can do you rapiers, or rape, or both, by all means faithless wives and ravished virgins – flagrante delicto at a price – for which there are special terms. It costs little to watch, and a little more to get caught up in the action – if that's your taste and times being what they are.

GUILDENSTERN: What are they?

PLAYER: Indifferent.

ROSENCRANTZ: Bad?

PLAYER: Wicked. See anything you like?

TRAGEDIANS
Posed again, not gallantly this time, provocatively, lewdly.

GUILDENSTERN *is tense, repelled.*

GUILDENSTERN: (*To* PLAYER) It was luck, then?

PLAYER: Or fate.

GUILDENSTERN: Yours or ours?

PLAYER: It could hardly be one without the other.

GUILDENSTERN: Fate then.

PLAYER: Oh, yes.

GUILDENSTERN: You said – caught up in the action.

PLAYER: I did, I did! You're quicker than your friend. Now for a handful of coins I happen to have a private and uncut performance of *The Rape of the Sabine Women* – or rather *Woman*, or rather Alfred – and for eight you can participate – taking either part.

(GUILDENSTERN *draws his sword halfway.* ROSENCRANTZ *does likewise.*)

TRAGEDIANS
Coming out of their poses.

GUILDENSTERN: It could have been – it didn't have to be *obscene*. I was *prepared*. But it's this, is it? – no enigma, no dignity, nothing classical, poetic – only this, a comic pornographer and a rabble of prostitutes.

PLAYER: You should have caught us in better times. We were purists then.

(*He bows, ironically, turns away. The* TRAGEDIANS *give up, turning away.*)

ROSENCRANTZ
Understands at last.

ROSENCRANTZ: Excuse me!

(*His tone is unmistakable.*)

PLAYER: Alfred.

(*Alfred turns back again.*

ROSENCRANTZ *climbs up on to the stage to join the* TRAGEDIANS.)

ROSENCRANTZ: You're not – ah – exclusively players, then?

PLAYER: We're inclusively players, sir.

ROSENCRANTZ: So you give – exhibitions?

PLAYER: Performances.

ROSENCRANTZ: Yes. You know, I had no idea –

PLAYER: No.

ROSENCRANTZ: I mean, I've *heard* of – but I've never actually –

PLAYER: No.

ROSENCRANTZ: I mean, what exactly do you do?

PLAYER: We keep to our usual stuff, more or less, only inside
out. We do on stage the things that are supposed to happen
off. Which is a kind of integrity, if you look on every exit as
being an entrance somewhere else.
(*The* TRAGEDIANS, *losing interest, are moving out of sight,
passing through the curtain concealing the interior stage.*)

ROSENCRANTZ: Just a minute! I wouldn't mind seeing – just an
idea of the kind of –
(*He walks the boards, embarrassed, making a distance between
himself and the* PLAYER. *He produces a coin. He spins it in the
air, towards the* PLAYER. *While it's in the air –*)
What will you do for that?

COIN
Falling, hitting the boards, spinning on the wood.

THE PLAYER
Stooping for the coin, which is still spinning on the wood.

THE COIN SPINNING
Before it stops spinning, a boot clamps down on it –
GUILDENSTERN's *boot.*

GUILDENSTERN: Do you know any good plays?

PLAYER: Plays? Oh, yes.

GUILDENSTERN: One of the Greeks, perhaps? You're familiar
with the tragedies of antiquity, are you? The great
homicidal classics? Maidens aspiring to godheads, and vice
versa? Your kind of thing, is it?

PLAYER: No, I can't say it is, really. We're more of the blood,
love and rhetoric school. Well, we can do you blood and
love without the rhetoric, and we can do you blood and
rhetoric without the love, and we can do you all three
concurrent or consecutive, but we can't do you love and
rhetoric without the blood. Blood is compulsory. They're all
blood, you see.

GUILDENSTERN: Is that what people want?

PLAYER: It's what we do.
(*The torches are still alight and dusk is falling.*

GUILDENSTERN *glances towards –*
The horses waiting.
He still has his foot on the coin.)
GUILDENSTERN: Do you like a bet? (*Indicating his foot.*) Double
or nothing.
PLAYER: Heads.
(GUILDENSTERN *raises his foot.*
The PLAYER *picks up the coin and turns away to go behind
the curtain.*)

ROSENCRANTZ
Spins a coin high.
ROSENCRANTZ: Heads!

COIN
Against darkening sky. The coin reaches the zenith and starts to fall.
Angle – floor. The coin hits, spins; ROSENCRANTZ's *boot clamps it
down.*
ROSENCRANTZ: Double or nothing.
(*He looks to the curtain.*
The PLAYER *gone.*
Angle – ROSENCRANTZ *and* GUILDENSTERN *alone on stage.*)
GUILDENSTERN: Come on.
(ROSENCRANTZ *stoops for the coin.*)
ROSENCRANTZ: I say – that was lucky. It was tails.
(*Sound: sobbing wail of a woman far off. Sound continues
through cut.*)

THE CURTAIN
Is still red but not tatty – we are at Elsinore.
OPHELIA – *in white like Alfred – bursts through the curtain,
wailing, sobbing, running . . .*
She is barefoot, white-gowned, hair like Alfred's wig.
Cut to –

INT. ELSINORE, DAY
The Painted Hall.
OPHELIA *is running from* HAMLET, *who also bursts through the
curtain, so wildly that he pulls the curtain down.*
It falls over the heads of ROSENCRANTZ *and* GUILDENSTERN.

HAMLET *catching up with* OPHELIA, *taking her by the wrist . . .
and (to quote Shakespeare) 'with his other hand over his brow, falls
to such perusal of her face as he would draw it. At last, with a little
shaking of his arm, and thrice his hand waving up and down, he
raises a sigh so piteous and profound that it does seem to shatter all his
bulk and end his being. That done he lets her go', and runs away up
the hall.* OPHELIA *runs away also.*

ROSENCRANTZ AND GUILDENSTERN
Get free of the curtain.

  We haven't seen where HAMLET *and* OPHELIA *went; we didn't
see them go. But the hall is empty.*

  Loose pages of manuscript blow along the floor.

  ROSENCRANTZ *and* GUILDENSTERN *move further into the
Painted Hall. Now we can hear a distant buzz of conversation,
distant footsteps.*

  These sounds grow louder.

  ROSENCRANTZ *and* GUILDENSTERN *get ready to receive
whatever is coming.*

  The hubbub becomes loud and close.

THE COURT
Led by CLAUDIUS *and* GERTRUDE, *sweeps in.*

  CLAUDIUS *and* GERTRUDE *are attended by a retinue of
COURTIERS, including children, and pets. There is a* SECRETARY
waiting to receive dictation; there is a CLERIC *for religious
emergencies and a* PHYSICIAN *who gives* CLAUDIUS *tablets and a
drink to swallow them with.*

CLAUDIUS: Welcome,
      (ROSENCRANTZ *and* GUILDENSTERN *bow to him.*)
                  dear Rosencrantz . . . and Guildenstern.
    Moreover that we much did long to see you,
    The need we have to use you did provoke
    Our hasty sending. Something have you heard
    Of Hamlet's transformation: – so call it,
    Sith nor th'exterior nor the inward man
    Resembles that is was. What it should be,
    More than his father's death, that thus hath put him
    So much from th'understanding of himself,
    I cannot dream of. I entreat you both

That, being of so young days brought up with him,
And sith so neighbour'd to his youth and haviour,
That you vouchsafe your rest here in our court
Some little time, so by your companies
To draw him on to pleasures and to gather,
So much as from occasion you may glean,
Whether aught to us unknown afflicts him thus
That, open'd, lies within our remedy.

GERTRUDE: Good . . .
  (*Like* CLAUDIUS, *she's not sure which is which, so she*
  compromises)
          . . . gentlemen, he hath much talk'd of you,
And sure I am, two men there is not living
To whom he more adheres. If it will please you
To show us so much gentry and good will
As to expend your time with us awhile
For the supply and profit of our hope,
Your visitation shall receive such thanks
As fits a king's remembrance.

ROSENCRANTZ: Both your Majesties
Might, by the sovereign power you have of us,
Put your dread pleasures more into command
Than to entreaty.

GUILDENSTERN: But we both obey,
And here give up ourselves in the full bent
To lay our service freely at your feet
To be commanded.

CLAUDIUS: Thanks, Rosencrantz and gentle Guildenstern.

GERTRUDE: (*Correcting him*) Thanks, Guildenstern and gentle
          Rosencrantz.
And I beseech you instantly to visit
My too much changed son.

(*The entire Shakespearean scene has taken place on the travel*
down the length of the Painted Hall, and CLAUDIUS *and*
GERTRUDE *are now about to leave by the opposite door. The*
fallen curtain is still on the floor next to this door but does not
impede the exits.)

GUILDENSTERN: Heaven make our presence and our practices

15

Pleasant and helpful to him!

GERTRUDE: Ay, amen.

(*And the entire court follows the* KING *and* QUEEN *out. The sound recedes.*)

ROSENCRANTZ: I want to go home.

GUILDENSTERN: Don't let them confuse you.

ROSENCRANTZ: We're in over our steps – heading out of depth – stepping out of our heads – it's all heading to a death –

(GUILDENSTERN *seizes him, shakes him.*)

GUILDENSTERN: There!

(*Startled by the echo, they whisper to each other.*)

Hasn't it ever happened to you that all of a sudden and for no reason at all you haven't the faintest idea how to spell the word 'which' . . . or 'house' . . . because when you write it down you just can't remember ever having seen those letters in that order before?

ROSENCRANTZ: I remember –

GUILDENSTERN: Yes?

ROSENCRANTZ: I remember when there were no questions.

GUILDENSTERN: There were always questions.

ROSENCRANTZ: Answers, yes. There were answers to everything.

GUILDENSTERN: You've forgotten.

ROSENCRANTZ: I haven't forgotten – how I used to remember my own name! And yours, oh, yes! There were answers everywhere you *looked*. There was no question about it – people knew who we were and if they didn't they asked and we told them our names.

(OSRIC *is way down the hall, at the lower door. With his hat he invites* ROSENCRANTZ *and* GUILDENSTERN *to follow him, and he goes out.*

They follow him.)

GUILDENSTERN: We did. The trouble is, each of them is . . . plausible, without being instinctive. All your life you live so close to truth, it becomes a permanent blur in the corner of your eye, and when something nudges it into outline it is like being ambushed by a grotesque. A man standing in his saddle in the half-lit, half-alive dawn banged on the shutters

and called two names. And when he called we came. That
much is certain – we came.
(*And they leave, following* OSRIC.)

INT. STAIRCASE
OSRIC *is disappearing round the corner ahead of them.*
  ROSENCRANTZ *and* GUILDENSTERN *follow up the stairs.*
ROSENCRANTZ: Well, I can tell you I'm sick to death of it. I
    don't care which one I am, so why don't you make up your
    mind?
GUILDENSTERN: We didn't come all this way for a christening.
    But we are comparatively fortunate – we might have been
    left to sift the whole field of human nomenclature like two
    blind men looting a bazaar for their own portraits . . . at
    least we are presented with alternatives.
ROSENCRANTZ: Well, as from now –
GUILDENSTERN: But not choice. Your smallest action sets off
    another somewhere else, and is set off by it. Keep an eye
    open, an ear cocked. Tread warily, follow instructions.
    We'll be all right.
    (*They reach the top of the staircase.*)

INT. THE PAINTED HALL
ROSENCRANTZ *and* GUILDENSTERN *enter at one of the upper
doors.*
ROSENCRANTZ: We're going round in circles.
    (CLAUDIUS *and* POLONIUS *are in conversation at the far end.*)
POLONIUS: . . . that I have found
    The very cause of Hamlet's lunacy!
CLAUDIUS: O speak of that: that do I long to hear.
    (POLONIUS *leaves.* GERTRUDE *enters. She and* CLAUDIUS
    *come along the length of the hall. He takes off his crown and
    tosses it to her.*)
    He tells me, my dear Gertrude, he hath found
    The head and source of all your son's distemper.
GERTRUDE: I doubt it is no other but the main,
    His father's death and our o'er-hasty marriage.
CLAUDIUS: Well, we shall sift him.
    (ROSENCRANTZ *and* GUILDENSTERN *watch them leave.*

They consider the Painted Hall. They are puzzled.
They come down the interior steps.)

GUILDENSTERN: There's a logic at work. It's all done for you, don't worry. Enjoy it. Relax.

(ROSENCRANTZ *nods.*
Pause.
They make a break for the door – the same door by which they had earlier left the same room.)

INT. SAME STAIRCASE
They are retracing their steps.

GUILDENSTERN: We have been briefed.

ROSENCRANTZ: Have we?

GUILDENSTERN: Hamlet's transformation. What do you recollect?

ROSENCRANTZ: Well, he's changed, hasn't he? The exterior and inward man fails to resemble –

GUILDENSTERN: Draw him on to pleasures – glean what afflicts him.

ROSENCRANTZ: Something more than his father's death –

GUILDENSTERN: He's always talking about us – there aren't two people living whom he dotes on more than us.

ROSENCRANTZ: We cheer him up – find out what's the matter –

GUILDENSTERN: Exactly.

(*They pause on the stairs.*)

It's a matter of asking the right questions and giving away as little as we can.

ROSENCRANTZ: And then we can go?

GUILDENSTERN: And receive such thanks as fits a king's remembrance.

ROSENCRANTZ: What did she mean by remembrance?

GUILDENSTERN: He doesn't forget his friends.

ROSENCRANTZ: Would you care to estimate?

GUILDENSTERN: Some kings tend to be . . . amnesiac, others I suppose the opposite, whatever that is . . .

ROSENCRANTZ: How much?

GUILDENSTERN: Elephantine.

ROSENCRANTZ: *How* much?

GUILDENSTERN: *Retentive* – he's a very retentive king, a royal
    retainer.
    (GUILDENSTERN *breaks away and continues down the stairs,
    followed by* ROSENCRANTZ.)
ROSENCRANTZ: What are you playing at?
GUILDENSTERN: Words. Words. They're all we have to go on.

INT. BADMINTON COURT AND GALLERY
ROSENCRANTZ *and* GUILDENSTERN *come through the door. They
both look surprised.*
    They are on a gallery.

GUILDENSTERN
*Exploring the badminton court, has reached the stairs leading down to
the body of the court.*
    The floor is marked out for badminton. There is a sagging net.
    *On the gallery there is a chest, a fairly large wooden box,
containing clutter to do with badminton, croquet and other games.*
ROSENCRANTZ'*s interest is caught by the stuff in the chest. He takes
out a croquet ball . . . a tennis ball . . . an Indian club . . .*
    In a casual sort of way he thinks he might try juggling.

GUILDENSTERN
Looks back towards ROSENCRANTZ.

ROSENCRANTZ
Attempts to juggle. All the objects hit the floor.
GUILDENSTERN: Leave things *alone!*
ROSENCRANTZ: Sorry.
    (ROSENCRANTZ *picks up an Indian club and a shuttlecock.*
    He tosses the objects back into the chest.
        ROSENCRANTZ *is intrigued. He picks up the club and the
shuttlecock and drops them together.*
    They fall together.
    *He is even more intrigued. He is within an ace of getting there
in front of Galileo. He finds a loose feather and a croquet ball in
the box and approaches the edge of the gallery.*)
    This is interesting. You would think that *this* (*the croquet
ball*) would fall faster than *this* (*the feather*) . . . wouldn't
    you?

(GUILDENSTERN *comes forward to watch the experiment.*
ROSENCRANTZ *drops the ball and the feather. The ball*
plummets, the feather floats down.)
And you'd be absolutely right.

ROSENCRANTZ
Comes down the steps to join GUILDENSTERN *in the body of the*
court.
They are on either side of the badminton net.
ROSENCRANTZ: Fancy a game?
GUILDENSTERN: We're spectators.
ROSENCRANTZ: Do you want to play questions?
GUILDENSTERN: How do you play that?
ROSENCRANTZ: You have to ask questions.
GUILDENSTERN: Statement! One–love.
ROSENCRANTZ: Cheating!
GUILDENSTERN: How?
ROSENCRANTZ: I hadn't started yet.
GUILDENSTERN: Statement! Two–love.
ROSENCRANTZ: Are you counting that?
GUILDENSTERN: What?
ROSENCRANTZ: Are you counting that?
GUILDENSTERN: Foul! No repetitions. Three–love and game.
ROSENCRANTZ: I'm not going to play if you're going to be like
    that.
    (*They change ends.*)
GUILDENSTERN: Whose serve?
ROSENCRANTZ: Er . . .
GUILDENSTERN: Hesitation! Love–one.
ROSENCRANTZ: Whose go?
GUILDENSTERN: Why?
ROSENCRANTZ: Why not?
GUILDENSTERN: What for?
ROSENCRANTZ: Foul! No synonyms! One–all.
GUILDENSTERN: What in God's name is going on?
ROSENCRANTZ: Foul! No rhetoric! Two–one.
GUILDENSTERN: What does it all add up to?
ROSENCRANTZ: Can't you guess?
GUILDENSTERN: Were you addressing me?

ROSENCRANTZ: Is there anyone else?

GUILDENSTERN: Who?

ROSENCRANTZ: How would I know?

GUILDENSTERN: Why do you ask?

ROSENCRANTZ: Are you serious?

GUILDENSTERN: Was that rhetoric?

ROSENCRANTZ: No.

GUILDENSTERN: Statement! Two all. Game point.

ROSENCRANTZ: What's the matter with you today?

GUILDENSTERN: When?

ROSENCRANTZ: What?

GUILDENSTERN: Are you deaf?

ROSENCRANTZ: Am I dead?

GUILDENSTERN: Yes or no?

ROSENCRANTZ: Is there a choice?

GUILDENSTERN: Is there a God?

ROSENCRANTZ: Foul! No *non sequiturs!* Three–two, one game all.

GUILDENSTERN: What's your name?

ROSENCRANTZ: What's yours?

GUILDENSTERN: You first.

ROSENCRANTZ: Statement! One–love.

GUILDENSTERN: What's your name when you're at home?

ROSENCRANTZ: What's yours?

GUILDENSTERN: When I'm at home?

ROSENCRANTZ: Is it different at home?

GUILDENSTERN: What home?

ROSENCRANTZ: Haven't you got one?

GUILDENSTERN: Why do you ask?

ROSENCRANTZ: What are you driving at?

GUILDENSTERN: What's your name?

ROSENCRANTZ: Repetition! Two–love. Match point.

   (*At the net:*)

GUILDENSTERN: (*Shouts*) Who do you think you are?

ROSENCRANTZ: Rhetoric! Game and match!

   (*He freezes, listening.*

     Sound off screen: the iron clank associated with the PLAYER's *cart, somewhere outside.*

     GUILDENSTERN *runs up the steps to the gallery.*

He goes to open a little window.

He sees the cart, drawn by the two horses, attended as before by the TRAGEDIANS.)

GUILDENSTERN: (*Without thought*) Rosencrantz!

ROSENCRANTZ: (*Without thought*) What?

(*They've cracked it!*)

GUILDENSTERN: There! How was that?

ROSENCRANTZ: Clever.

GUILDENSTERN: Natural?

ROSENCRANTZ: Instinctive!

(*They are delighted, relieved.*)

Now I'll try you! Guil–

GUILDENSTERN: Not yet! Catch me unawares!

ROSENCRANTZ: Right!

(*He strolls away. He whistles quietly to himself.*)

(*Side of mouth*) Ready?

GUILDENSTERN: Never mind.

(*He leaves the gallery through the opposite door.*)

INT. CORRIDOR

But it is a different kind of corridor, a place of echoing footsteps and shafts of light. The light comes piercing through grilles in the walls.

GUILDENSTERN *pauses, listening.*

POLONIUS: I have a daughter – have while she is mine –

Who in her duty and obedience, mark,

Hath given me this. Now gather and surmise.

(GUILDENSTERN *follows the voice towards a lighted grille. He sees* POLONIUS *reading a letter aloud, to* CLAUDIUS *and* GERTRUDE.)

'To the celestial and my soul's idol,

the most beautified Ophelia . . .'

(*They are moving up a staircase. Their progress crosses* GUILDENSTERN's *view on the upward diagonal.*)

– That's an ill phrase, a vile phrase,

'beautified' is a vile phrase.

But you shall hear – 'these; in

her excellent white bosom . . .'

GERTRUDE: Came this from Hamlet to her?

(*They pass by upward and out of earshot.*

GUILDENSTERN *hears a bird start to sing quietly . . . and then he hears a cuckoo . . . a dog . . . a cow . . . by which time he has turned and retraced his steps and discovered these noises coming from* ROSENCRANTZ *who is solemnly doing animal impressions.* GUILDENSTERN *patiently discourages* ROSENCRANTZ, *who desists.* ROSENCRANTZ *follows* GUILDENSTERN *back to another lighted grille beyond which* POLONIUS *and* GERTRUDE *are continuing their scene as they move up the staircase.*)

INT. CORRIDOR. CONTINUATION
POLONIUS, CLAUDIUS *and* GERTRUDE *appear at the end of the corridor,* POLONIUS *still telling his tale.*
POLONIUS: And my young mistress thus I did bespeak:
'Lord Hamlet is a prince out of thy star.
This must not be.'

INT. CHAMBER
GUILDENSTERN *is on a gallery.*
He looks down into the body of the room.
HAMLET *is crossing the chamber.*
There is a harp standing in the room and the draught ripples the strings quietly. HAMLET *is alerted to* POLONIUS's *approach, and he picks up a book.*
POLONIUS *enters the chamber.*
POLONIUS: How does my good Lord Hamlet?
HAMLET: Well, God-a-mercy.
POLONIUS: Do you know me, my lord?
HAMLET: Excellent well. You are a fishmonger.
POLONIUS: Not I, my lord.
(*They leave through a door, continuing their scene.*
GUILDENSTERN *is joined by* ROSENCRANTZ.)

INT/EXT. CLOISTER
GUILDENSTERN *and* ROSENCRANTZ *can hear voices from beneath their feet.*
POLONIUS: What do you read, my lord?
HAMLET: Words, words, words.
POLONIUS: What is the matter, my lord?

HAMLET: Between who?
POLONIUS: I mean the matter that you read, my lord.
ROSENCRANTZ: (*Quietly*) Statement.
  (GUILDENSTERN *not amused*.)

INT/EXT. CLOISTER
They come down the stairs. Now they are in the ground-floor cloister. They begin to walk.
ROSENCRANTZ: Who was that?
GUILDENSTERN: Didn't you know him?
ROSENCRANTZ: He didn't know me.
GUILDENSTERN: He didn't see you.
ROSENCRANTZ: I didn't see him.
GUILDENSTERN: We shall see. I *hardly* knew him, he's changed.
ROSENCRANTZ: You could see that?
GUILDENSTERN: Transformed.
ROSENCRANTZ: How do you know?
GUILDENSTERN: Inside and out.
ROSENCRANTZ: I see.
GUILDENSTERN: He's not himself.
ROSENCRANTZ: He's changed.
GUILDENSTERN: I could see that. Glean what afflicts him!
ROSENCRANTZ: Me?
GUILDENSTERN: Him.
ROSENCRANTZ: How?
GUILDENSTERN: Question and answer.
ROSENCRANTZ: He's afflicted.
GUILDENSTERN: You question, I'll answer.
ROSENCRANTZ: He's not himself, you know.
GUILDENSTERN: I'm him, you see.
ROSENCRANTZ: Who am I?
GUILDENSTERN: You're yourself.
ROSENCRANTZ: And he's you?
GUILDENSTERN: Not a bit of it.
ROSENCRANTZ: Are *you* afflicted?
GUILDENSTERN: That's the idea. Are you ready?
ROSENCRANTZ: Let's go back a bit.
GUILDENSTERN: I'm afflicted.
ROSENCRANTZ: I see.

GUILDENSTERN: Glean what afflicts me.
ROSENCRANTZ: Right.
GUILDENSTERN: Question and answer.
ROSENCRANTZ: How should I begin?
GUILDENSTERN: Address me.
  (GUILDENSTERN *leans on a pillar, Hamlet-like.*)
ROSENCRANTZ: My dear Guildenstern!
  (GUILDENSTERN *breaks his pose.*)
GUILDENSTERN: You've forgotten, haven't you?
ROSENCRANTZ: My dear Rosencrantz!
GUILDENSTERN: I don't think you quite understand. What we
  are attempting is a hypothesis in which *I* answer for *him*
  while *you* ask me questions.
ROSENCRANTZ: Ah! Ready?
GUILDENSTERN: You know what to do?
ROSENCRANTZ: What?
GUILDENSTERN: Are you stupid?
ROSENCRANTZ: Pardon?
GUILDENSTERN: Are you deaf?
ROSENCRANTZ: Did you speak?
GUILDENSTERN: Not now –
ROSENCRANTZ: Statement!
GUILDENSTERN: (*Shouts*) Not now!
  (GUILDENSTERN'*s shout echoes around.*)

EXT. ELSINORE
The PLAYER *looks up, hearing the echo.*
  The other TRAGEDIANS *also look up; they are unloading the cart.*

THE CLOISTER
ROSENCRANTZ *and* GUILDENSTERN, *frightened, hurrying away.*
  Cut to –

EXT. GARDEN, DAY
They are entering a garden.
  The garden. Trees. Flowers. An ornamental well.
  An apple falls from above, landing squarely on ROSENCRANTZ'*s
head and bouncing off.* ROSENCRANTZ *looks up.*
  The brightly laden boughs of the apple tree are above him.

ROSENCRANTZ *considers the tree above. He considers the apple lying on the ground. He has a thought.*

ROSENCRANTZ: I say . . .

GUILDENSTERN: What?

ROSENCRANTZ: Well . . . !

(GUILDENSTERN *stares at him sceptically.* ROSENCRANTZ *abandons the thought. He offers the apple to* GUILDENSTERN.) Would you like a bite?

GUILDENSTERN: No, thank you.

(GUILDENSTERN *retires and sits down on a stone bench.*
ROSENCRANTZ *takes a bite of the apple. He thinks deeply. He has another thought.*)

ROSENCRANTZ: Ohhh . . . you mean – you pretend to be *him*, and I ask you questions!

GUILDENSTERN: Very good.

ROSENCRANTZ: You had me confused.

GUILDENSTERN: I could see I had.

ROSENCRANTZ: How should I begin?

GUILDENSTERN: Address me.

(GUILDENSTERN *gets into his Hamlet pose.* ROSENCRANTZ *gets ready.*)

ROSENCRANTZ: My honoured lord!

GUILDENSTERN: My dear Rosencrantz!

ROSENCRANTZ: Am I pretending to be you, then?

GUILDENSTERN: Certainly not. If you like. Shall we continue?

ROSENCRANTZ: Question and answer.

GUILDENSTERN: Right.

ROSENCRANTZ: Right. My honoured lord!

GUILDENSTERN: My dear fellow!

ROSENCRANTZ: How are you?

GUILDENSTERN: Afflicted!

ROSENCRANTZ: Really? In what way?

GUILDENSTERN: Transformed.

ROSENCRANTZ: Inside or out?

GUILDENSTERN: Both.

ROSENCRANTZ: I see. Not much new there.

GUILDENSTERN: (*Shouts*) Go into details. *Delve.*

(GUILDENSTERN'S *shout brings* OPHELIA *to a window.*) Probe the background, establish the situation.

26

ROSENCRANTZ: So – so your uncle is the King of Denmark?!

GUILDENSTERN: And my father before him.

ROSENCRANTZ: His father before him?

GUILDENSTERN: No, *my* father before him.

ROSENCRANTZ: But surely –

GUILDENSTERN: You might well ask.

ROSENCRANTZ: Let me get it straight. Your father was king. You were his only son. Your father dies. You are of age. Your uncle becomes king.

GUILDENSTERN: Yes.

ROSENCRANTZ: Unusual.

GUILDENSTERN: Undid me.

ROSENCRANTZ: Undeniable.

GUILDENSTERN: He slipped in.

ROSENCRANTZ: Which reminds me.

GUILDENSTERN: Well, it would.

ROSENCRANTZ: I don't want to be personal.

GUILDENSTERN: It's common knowledge.

ROSENCRANTZ: Your mother's marriage.

GUILDENSTERN: He slipped in.

ROSENCRANTZ: (*Beat.*) His body was still warm.

GUILDENSTERN: So was hers.

ROSENCRANTZ: Extraordinary.

GUILDENSTERN: Indecent.

ROSENCRANTZ: Hasty.

GUILDENSTERN: Suspicious.

ROSENCRANTZ: It makes you think.

GUILDENSTERN: Don't think I haven't thought of it.

ROSENCRANTZ: And with her husband's brother.

GUILDENSTERN: They were close.

ROSENCRANTZ: She went to him.

GUILDENSTERN: Too close.

ROSENCRANTZ: For comfort.

GUILDENSTERN: It looks bad.

ROSENCRANTZ: It adds up.

GUILDENSTERN: Incest to adultery.

ROSENCRANTZ: Would you go so far?

GUILDENSTERN: Never!

ROSENCRANTZ: To sum up! Your father, whom you love, dies,

you are his heir, you come back to find that hardly was the corpse cold before his young brother popped on to his throne and into his sheets, thereby offending both legal and natural practice. Now – why exactly are you behaving in this extraordinary manner?

GUILDENSTERN: I can't imagine!

(GUILDENSTERN *comes out of his Hamlet pose.*)

And yet we were sent for. And we did come.

(ROSENCRANTZ *has made a discovery. Four or five spherical earthenware pots hang from a branch. They hang touching each other, forming a 'Newton's Cradle'. They hang from individual strings.*

ROSENCRANTZ *gives the first pot a little swing and finds that the one at the far end is nudged out of position by the impact. He is definitely intrigued.*)

Rosencrantz.

ROSENCRANTZ: (*Preoccupied*) What?

GUILDENSTERN: Guildenstern.

ROSENCRANTZ: (*Still preoccupied doing his Newton trick*) What?

GUILDENSTERN: (*Angrily*) Don't you discriminate at all?

ROSENCRANTZ: (*Abandoning the Newton*) What?

GUILDENSTERN: Nothing!

ROSENCRANTZ: (*Returning to Newton*) Look at this.

(ROSENCRANTZ *attempts to demonstrate his discovery. But it lets him down. The pot disintegrates on impact.*)

GUILDENSTERN: Interesting.

INT. COBWEBBED DERELICT CHAMBER

HAMLET *crowing and clucking, squatting, waggling his elbows . . . Then – we see* HAMLET *is showing his book to a chicken.*

He clucks and crows.

POLONIUS *is watching him dubiously.*

POLONIUS: My lord, I will take my leave of you.

HAMLET: You cannot, sir, take from me anything that I will not more willingly part withal . . .

(*He crows and clucks.*)

– except my life . . .

(*He crows and clucks.*)

. . . except my life . . .

(POLONIUS *shakes his head sadly – the lunatic is clearly far gone.*)

. . . except my life.

(POLONIUS *retires hastily.*

In leaving, POLONIUS *sees that* ROSENCRANTZ *and* GUILDENSTERN *are watching* HAMLET, *from the door.*)

(*Quietly*) These tedious old fools!

(HAMLET *goes to a 'Hamlet's chair' and is evidently soliloquizing.*)

POLONIUS: You go to seek the Lord Hamlet. There he is.

ROSENCRANTZ: (*As* POLONIUS *walks by*) God save you, sir!

(POLONIUS *goes.* ROSENCRANTZ *and* GUILDENSTERN *peer at* HAMLET.)

What's he doing?

GUILDENSTERN: Talking.

(ROSENCRANTZ *moves for a better look.*)

To himself.

(ROSENCRANTZ *and* GUILDENSTERN *enter and bow.*)

My honoured lord!

ROSENCRANTZ: My most dear lord!

(HAMLET *turning to look at them, recognizing them, approaching them, delightedly.*)

HAMLET: My excellent good friends! (*To* ROSENCRANTZ) How dost thou, Guildenstern?

(*He looks at* GUILDENSTERN, *realizes he's got it wrong, looks back to* ROSENCRANTZ.)

Ah, Rosencrantz!

(*He makes up for the mistake with handshakes and hugs.*)

Good lads, how do you both?

(ROSENCRANTZ *and* GUILDENSTERN *look pleased and grateful.*)

ROSENCRANTZ: As the indifferent childen of the earth.

GUILDENSTERN: Happy in that we are not over-happy: on Fortune's cap we are not the very button.

HAMLET: Nor the soles of her shoes?

ROSENCRANTZ: Neither, my lord.

HAMLET: Then you live about her waist, or in the middle of her favours?

GUILDENSTERN: Faith, her privates we.

HAMLET: In the secret parts of Fortune? O most true, she is a strumpet. What news?

ROSENCRANTZ: None, my lord, but the world's grown honest.

HAMLET: Then is doomsday near. But your news is not true. Let me question more in particular. What have you, my good friends, deserved at the hands of Fortune that she sends you to prison hither?

GUILDENSTERN: Prison, my lord?

HAMLET: Denmark's a prison.

ROSENCRANTZ: Then is the world one.

HAMLET: A goodly one, in which there are many confines, wards, and dungeons, Denmark being one o'the' worst.

ROSENCRANTZ: We think not so, my lord.

HAMLET: Why, then 'tis none to you; for there is nothing either good or bad but thinking makes it so. To me it is a prison.

ROSENCRANTZ: Why, then your ambition makes it one: 'tis too narrow for your mind.

HAMLET: O God, I could be bounded in a nutshell and count myself a king of infinite space – were it not that I have bad dreams. But in the beaten way of friendship, what make you at Elsinore?

(*Angle* – ROSENCRANTZ *and* GUILDENSTERN: *they field the question, hesitate.*)

ROSENCRANTZ: To visit you, my lord, no other occasion.

(HAMLET *draws his sword.*)

HAMLET: Were you not sent for? Is it your own inclining? Is it a free visitation? Come, come. Nay, speak.

GUILDENSTERN: What should we say, my lord?

HAMLET: Anything – but to th' purpose. You were sent for. I know the good King and Queen have sent for you.

ROSENCRANTZ: To what end, my lord?

HAMLET: That, you must teach me. Be even and direct with me whether you were sent for or no.

GUILDENSTERN: My lord, we were sent for.

(HAMLET *triumphantly swings his sword . . .*
He slashes through the rope holding up a dusty iron chandelier which falls with a crash on to the table beneath.)

HAMLET: I will tell you why.
    (*The three of them take their seats at the table.*)

INT. DINING CHAMBER
*They appear to be in the same place, with the same furniture, but
everything is clean and tidy and quite luxurious. They are coming to
the end of a considerable meal.* HAMLET *has a cup-and-ball toy.*
ROSENCRANTZ *also has a toy. He has made a 'windmill' using an
apple-core, some bits of stick and some bits of paper to make sails. A
child's amusement.*

  ROSENCRANTZ *and* GUILDENSTERN *wait for* HAMLET *to speak.*
HAMLET *suddenly jumps up and stands on the table, declaiming like
an actor.*
HAMLET: 'Anon he finds him,
    Striking too short at Greeks . . .'
    (HAMLET *abandons the performance.*)
    I have of late, but wherefore I know not, lost all my
    mirth, forgone all custom of exercises; and indeed it goes
    so heavily with my disposition that this goodly frame the
    earth seems to me a sterile promontory, this most
    excellent canopy the air, look you, this brave o'erhanging
    firmament, this majestical roof fretted with golden fire,
    why, it appeareth nothing to me but a foul and pestilent
    congregation of vapours.
    (*By this time he has crawled along the table and got back to his
    chair. He picks up his cup and ball, and gives an occasional
    belch as he continues.*)
    What a piece of work is a man, how noble in reason, how
    infinite in faculties, in form and moving how express and
    admirable, in action how like an angel, in apprehension
    how like a god: the beauty of the world, the paragon of
    animals – and yet, to me, what is this quintessence of
    dust? Man delights not me – nor woman either, though
    by your smiling you seem to say so.
ROSENCRANTZ: My lord, there was no such stuff in my
    thoughts.
HAMLET: Why did ye laugh then, when I said man delights not
    me?
ROSENCRANTZ: To think, my lord, if you delight not in man,

what Lenten entertainment the players shall receive from you. We coted them on the way, and hither are they coming to offer you service.

HAMLET: He that plays the king shall be welcome.

(*He pushes back his chair, staggers to his feet.*)

Gentlemen, you are welcome to Elsinore. Your hands, come then.

(*He takes their hands and leans blurrily into* ROSENCRANTZ *and* GUILDENSTERN.)

You are welcome. By my uncle-father and aunt-mother are deceived.

GUILDENSTERN: In what, my dear lord?

HAMLET: I am but mad north-north-west. When the wind is southerly I know a hawk from a handsaw.

(HAMLET *is gripping their hands so tightly that* ROSENCRANTZ *and* GUILDENSTERN *whimper with pain.*

POLONIUS *enters.*)

POLONIUS: Well be with you, gentlemen.

HAMLET: (*To* GUILDENSTERN) Hark you . . . (*Hesitates, trying to get the name right*) Guildenstern . . . (*To* ROSENCRANTZ) . . . and you too – at each ear a hearer. That great baby you see there is not yet out of his swaddling-clouts. I will prophesy he comes to tell me of the players.

POLONIUS: (*Approaching*) My lord, I have news to tell you.

HAMLET: (*Mimicking him*) My lord, I have news to tell you. When Roscius was an actor in Rome –

POLONIUS: The actors are come hither, my lord.

HAMLET: Buzz, buzz.

POLONIUS: Upon my honour –

HAMLET: Then came each actor on his ass –

(POLONIUS *is now hurrying off with* HAMLET.)

POLONIUS: The best actors in the world, either for tragedy, comedy, history, pastoral, pastoral-comical, historical-pastoral, tragical-historical, tragical-comical-historical-pastoral . . .

(POLONIUS's *voice continues, fading beyond the closed door.* ROSENCRANTZ *and* GUILDENSTERN *remain stranded. Pause.*)

32

GUILDENSTERN: Hm?
ROSENCRANTZ: Yes?
GUILDENSTERN: What?
ROSENCRANTZ: I thought you . . .
GUILDENSTERN: No.
ROSENCRANTZ: Ah.

(ROSENCRANTZ *turns his attention back to his windmill. He notices the steam coming from the kettle on the hob. He has yet another interesting thought. He takes his windmill to the fire and becomes busy behind* GUILDENSTERN'S *back.* GUILDENSTERN *decides to wash his hands in a bowl which is on the table but he finds that the water jug is empty.*)

Look at this . . .

(*We see what* ROSENCRANTZ *has done: adapting his windmill to steam power he has invented the Magimix. His invention turns merrily inside a pot on the flames.*

GUILDENSTERN, *coming to the kettle to get water, gathers up the whole contraption inadvertently, not noticing the now ruined Magimix until he has put the kettle on the table. He is puzzled for a moment, but disentangles* ROSENCRANTZ'S *invention and throws it on the ground, then begins to wash his hands.*

ROSENCRANTZ *resignedly picks up his bits and pieces.*

GUILDENSTERN *completes his ablutions.*)

GUILDENSTERN: I think we can say we made some progress.
ROSENCRANTZ: You think so?
GUILDENSTERN: I think we can say that.
ROSENCRANTZ: I think we can say he made us look ridiculous.
GUILDENSTERN: We played it close to the chest of course.
ROSENCRANTZ: 'Question and answer!' He was scoring off us all down the line.
GUILDENSTERN: He caught us on the wrong foot once or twice, perhaps, but I thought we gained some ground.
ROSENCRANTZ: He murdered us.
GUILDENSTERN: He might have had the edge.
ROSENCRANTZ: Twenty-seven–three, and you think he might have had the edge? He *murdered* us.
GUILDENSTERN: What about our evasions?
ROSENCRANTZ: Oh, our evasions were lovely. 'Were you sent

for?' 'My lord, we were sent for.' I didn't know where to put myself.

GUILDENSTERN: He had six rhetoricals –

ROSENCRANTZ: It was question and answer, all right. Twenty-seven questions he got out and answered three. I was waiting for you to *delve*. When is he going to start *delving*, I asked myself.

GUILDENSTERN: And two repetitions.

ROSENCRANTZ: Hardly a leading question between us.

GUILDENSTERN: We got his symptoms, didn't we?

ROSENCRANTZ: Half of what he said meant something else, and the other half didn't mean anything at all.

GUILDENSTERN: Thwarted ambition – a sense of grievance, that's my diagnosis.

(ROSENCRANTZ *is still busy, and we have gathered that whatever he's doing he is doing it with the toy windmill.*)

ROSENCRANTZ: Six rhetorical and two repetition, leaving nineteen, of which we answered fifteen. And what did we get in return? He's depressed! Denmark's a prison and he'd rather live in a nutshell. Some shadowplay about the nature of ambition and finally one direct question which might have led somewhere and led in fact to his illuminating claim to tell a hawk from a handbag.

GUILDENSTERN: Handsaw. When the wind is southerly.

ROSENCRANTZ: And the weather's clear.

GUILDENSTERN: And when it isn't he can't.

ROSENCRANTZ: He's at the mercy of the elements.

(*A door slams loudly. Candle flames on the table flare sideways. They look in the direction of the door-slam.*)

Is that southerly?

GUILDENSTERN: It doesn't look southerly. What made you think so?

ROSENCRANTZ: I didn't say I think so. It could be northerly for all I know.

GUILDENSTERN: We came from roughly south.

ROSENCRANTZ: Which way is that?

(GUILDENSTERN *looks around, clears his throat, takes charge.*)

GUILDENSTERN: In the morning the sun would be easterly. I think we can assume that.

ROSENCRANTZ: That it's morning?

GUILDENSTERN: If it is, and the sun is over *there*, for instance, *that* would be northerly. On the other hand, if it is not morning and the sun in over *there* . . . *that* . . . would still be northerly. To put it another way, if we came from down there, and it is morning, the sun would be up there . . . and if it is actually over *there*, and it's still morning, we must have come from back *there* . . . and if *that* is southerly, and the sun is really over *there* . . . then it's the afternoon. However, if none of these is the case –

ROSENCRANTZ: Why don't you go and have a look?

GUILDENSTERN: Pragmatism! – Is that all you have to offer?

ROSENCRANTZ: I merely suggest that the position of the sun, if it is out, would give you a rough idea of the time. Alternatively, the clock, if it is going, would give you a rough idea of the position of the sun. I forget what you are trying to establish.

GUILDENSTERN: I am trying to establish the direction of the wind.

ROSENCRANTZ: There isn't any wind.

(But by now he has turned his Magimix into a windmill on a stick . . . and the windmill is revolving.)

Draught, yes.

(The draught becomes stronger and the windmill whizzes round at speed and their hair is blown by the draught.

And now they begin to hear a voice declaiming from somewhere far off in the castle.)

PLAYER: Anon he finds him,

Striking too short at Greeks.

STAIRCASE

ROSENCRANTZ *and* GUILDENSTERN *hurry down towards the voice which continues, echoing around them. On a landing they find a small window and looking through they find they are looking from above into a large kitchen . . . in which the* PLAYER, *standing on a table, is declaiming. His audience includes* HAMLET *and* POLONIUS, *and the* TRAGEDIANS.

PLAYER: Out, out, thou strumpet Fortune! All you gods,

In general synod take away her power,

35

Break all the spokes and fellies from her wheel,
And bowl the round nave down the hill of heaven . . .

INT. STAIRCASE
ROSENCRANTZ *and* GUILDENSTERN *continue to hurry down the stairs. They reach a landing.*
GUILDENSTERN: Mind the bottom . . .
   (ROSENCRANTZ *trips over the bottom step and falls heavily.*)
   . . . step.
ROSENCRANTZ: (*Picking himself up*) Sorry.
   (*They are on a landing which incorporates a trapdoor operated by ropes. The* PLAYER'*s performance continues to be heard from the unseen kitchen below. There is a covered drainpipe against the wall.* GUILDENSTERN *puts his ear to the drainpipe, to listen all the better. Meanwhile,* ROSENCRANTZ *has discovered the trapdoor. He pulls one of the ropes and the trapdoor hinges open, revealing a chute evidently used for delivering supplies to the kitchen.* ROSENCRANTZ *pulls the rope which closes the trapdoor. The trapdoor obviously works on a system of counter-balance.* ROSENCRANTZ *steps tentatively on to the trapdoor, holding the rope tight to prevent the trapdoor opening under his feet.*)
I say, this in interesting.
   (GUILDENSTERN *is still listening to the drainpipe. The voice from below distorts as water gurgles down the pipe, and* GUILDENSTERN *slaps the drainpipe, and the voice comes into clear again. The scene taking place below is from Hamlet, Act II Scene ii.*)

INT. KITCHEN
PLAYER: . . . would have made milch the burning eyes of heaven
      And passion in the gods.
POLONIUS: Look, whe'er he has not turned his colour and has
      tears in's eyes. Prithee no more.
HAMLET: 'Tis well. I'll have thee speak out the rest of this soon.

ON THE LANDING
GUILDENSTERN *joins* ROSENCRANTZ *on the trapdoor, kneeling down to put his ear to the floor. The extra weight puts*

36

ROSENCRANTZ *in difficulties. He signals urgently to*
GUILDENSTERN *but* GUILDENSTERN *shushes him up.*

INT. KITCHEN
HAMLET: Good my lord, will you see the players well bestowed?
    Do you hear, let them be well used, for they are the
    abstract and brief chronicles of the time. After your death
    you were better have a bad epitaph than their ill report
    while you live.
POLONIUS: My lord, I will use them according to their desert.

ON THE LANDING
ROSENCRANTZ *is having difficulty keeping the trapdoor shut. It
doesn't occur to him to step off it.* HAMLET's *voice continues from
below.*

INT. KITCHEN
HAMLET: (*To* PLAYER) Dost thou hear me, old friend? Can you
    play *The Murder of Gonzago?*
PLAYER: Ay, my lord.
HAMLET: We'll ha't tomorrow night. You could for a need study
    a speech of some dozen or sixteen lines, which I would set
    down and insert in't, could you not?
PLAYER: Ay, my lord.

ON THE LANDING
ROSENCRANTZ *lets go of the rope and the two of them fall down the
chute.*

INT. KITCHEN
HAMLET: Very well. Follow that lord, and look you mock him
    not.
    (*The* PLAYER *bows and leaves.*
    The chute leads to a large wooden bin in the kitchen.
    HAMLET *raises the lid of the bin.* ROSENCRANTZ *and*
    GUILDENSTERN *are tumbled about inside.*)
    My good friends, I'll leave you till night. You are
    welcome to Elsinore.
ROSENCRANTZ: Good my lord.
    (HAMLET *lets the lid of the bin slam shut.*)

37

BLACKNESS

INT. BATH HOUSE, DAY
The bath house is full of unidentified people washing and towelling.

    ROSENCRANTZ's *head emerges from under the surface of a big tub of water. He had made himself a little paper boat.*

    GUILDENSTERN *is already dressed after his bath. He is cleaning his teeth with a stick, looking into a mirror.*

    ROSENCRANTZ *raises himself out of his bath but then notices that in so doing he has lowered the water level as indicated by his toy boat floating on the surface. He lowers himself back into the water and the boat rises up to the scum mark.* ROSENCRANTZ *raises himself again and the boat lowers. He is about to rediscover Archimedes' Principle. But before he can announce his discovery his attention is caught by what he takes to be a half-naked woman, seen from behind. Then he realizes that the woman is Alfred.*

    ROSENCRANTZ *looks about and in each case he finds that the other people in the bath house are the* TRAGEDIANS. *Finally, the* PLAYER *himself is revealed to* ROSENCRANTZ *in a cloud of steam. The* PLAYER *is dressed up in a Hamlet costume, and ultimately when we come to see all the* TRAGEDIANS *dressed we realize that they are clothed for a dress rehearsal of a play* (The Murder of Gonzago) *which is a blurred mirror image of the people and events at Elsinore.*

    Now GUILDENSTERN *also glimpses the* PLAYER *revealed in a cloud of steam.*

    GUILDENSTERN *walks through the bath house, looking for the* PLAYER, *who has disappeared again. He finally catches up with the* PLAYER *in an area of clothes racks on which hang various costumes.*

GUILDENSTERN: So you've caught up.

PLAYER: Not yet, sir.

GUILDENSTERN: Now mind your tongue, or we'll have it out and throw the rest of you away like a nightingale at a Roman feast.

    (ROSENCRANTZ, *almost dressed, appears from behind the hanging costumes.*)

ROSENCRANTZ: Took the words out of my mouth.

GUILDENSTERN: You'd be lost for words.

ROSENCRANTZ: You'd be tongue tied.

GUILDENSTERN: Like a mute in a monologue.

ROSENCRANTZ: Like a nightingale at a Roman feast.

PLAYER: You left us!

GUILDENSTERN: Yes . . . on the road . . . I'm sorry we . . .

PLAYER: You don't understand the humiliation of it. To be tricked out of the single assumption that makes our existence bearable; that somebody is watching.

GUILDENSTERN: We had an appointment.

PLAYER: That's true.

> (*He turns away.* ROSENCRANTZ *and* GUILDENSTERN *follow him.*
>
> Now they are in a 'white box' made up of white drapes which divide the bath house into cubicles.)

You know why you're here?

GUILDENSTERN: We only know what we're told and for all we know it isn't even true.

PLAYER: One acts on assumptions. What do you assume?

ROSENCRANTZ: Hamlet is not himself outside or in. We have to glean what afflicts him.

GUILDENSTERN: He's melancholy.

PLAYER: Melancholy?

GUILDENSTERN: Mad.

PLAYER: How is he mad?

ROSENCRANTZ: Ah. (*To* GUILDENSTERN) How is he mad?

GUILDENSTERN: More morose than mad perhaps.

PLAYER: Melancholy.

GUILDENSTERN: Moody.

ROSENCRANTZ: He has moods.

PLAYER: Of moroseness?

GUILDENSTERN: Madness and yet.

ROSENCRANTZ: Quite.

GUILDENSTERN: For instance.

ROSENCRANTZ: He talks to himself, which might be madness.

GUILDENSTERN: If he didn't talk sense, which he does.

ROSENCRANTZ: Which suggests the opposite.

PLAYER: Of what?

GUILDENSTERN: I think I have it. A man talking sense to himself is no madder than a man talking nonsense to himself.

ROSENCRANTZ: Or just as mad.

GUILDENSTERN: Or just as mad.

ROSENCRANTZ: And he does both.

GUILDENSTERN: So there you are.

ROSENCRANTZ: Start raving sane.

PLAYER: Why?

GUILDENSTERN: Ah. Why?

ROSENCRANTZ: Exactly.

GUILDENSTERN: Exactly what?

ROSENCRANTZ: Exactly why?

GUILDENSTERN: Exactly why what?

ROSENCRANTZ: What?

GUILDENSTERN: *Why?*

ROSENCRANTZ: Why what, exactly?

GUILDENSTERN: Why is he mad?

ROSENCRANTZ: *I* don't know!

PLAYER: The old man thinks he's in love with his daughter.

ROSENCRANTZ: Good God! We're out of our depth here!

PLAYER: No, no, no – *he* hasn't got a daughter – the old man thinks he's in love with *his* daughter.

ROSENCRANTZ: The old man is?

PLAYER: Hamlet. In love. With the old man's daughter. The old man thinks.

ROSENCRANTZ: Ha! It's beginning to make sense! Unrequited passion!

(ROSENCRANTZ *and* GUILDENSTERN *look around. The* PLAYER *has gone. They pull aside one of the hanging drapes.*

The TRAGEDIANS, *in rehearsal costume, are grouped together on a landing above the bath house, staring down at them. The* PLAYER *is walking along the landing to join them.*)

GUILDENSTERN: Where are you going?

PLAYER: I can come and go as I please.

GUILDENSTERN: You know your way around.

PLAYER: I've been here before.

GUILDENSTERN: We're still finding our feet.

PLAYER: I should concentrate on not losing your heads.

GUILDENSTERN: Do you speak from knowledge?

PLAYER: Precedent.

GUILDENSTERN: You've been here before.

PLAYER: And I know which way the wind is blowing.

WINE CELLAR
The TRAGEDIANS, *led by the* PLAYER, *march towards the camera,
along a passage between giant casks of wine. Behind them*
ROSENCRANTZ *and* GUILDENSTERN *hurry to catch up.*

BRICK CLOISTERS
The TRAGEDIANS *and* ROSENCRANTZ *and* GUILDENSTERN
*continue their march . . . but they have become separated and now
appear on different levels on the double-decked cloisters.*
ROSENCRANTZ *and* GUILDENSTERN *realize their mistake and hurry
back, reappearing on the lower level, as speedily as Keystone Kops
. . . finally reappearing in front of the camera just in time to see the
group of* TRAGEDIANS *reappear at speed in the cloister where we saw*
ROSENCRANTZ *and* GUILDENSTERN *in the first place.*
ROSENCRANTZ: This place is a madhouse.

INT. BARN
The TRAGEDIANS' *rehearsal is given to an audience of* SERVANTS,
*twenty or thirty peasants deployed among the tables, benches and
rafters. They are watching an enigmatic scene in which the* PLAYER
*(dressed more or less as Hamlet) is lying on a couch, playing a small
wood pipe. A* TRAGEDIAN, *dressed more or less as Polonius,
approaches 'Hamlet' and bows to him. However, the audience's
attention is distracted by the appearance of* ROSENCRANTZ *and*
GUILDENSTERN *at the back of the stage.* ROSENCRANTZ *and*
GUILDENSTERN *stare at the strange sight before them. The audience
hoots with laughter and the* PLAYER *realizes that something is
happening behind him. He stops playing and looks disapprovingly at*
ROSENCRANTZ *and* GUILDENSTERN, *who realize they are
interrupting some kind of play, and move out of sight.*
　　*The rehearsal continues with a version of Hamlet, Act III Scene
iv. 'Polonius' prepares 'Gertrude' for the arrival of 'Hamlet'. (All the
scenes are done in mime.) 'Polonius' hides behind the curtain.
'Hamlet' arrives and mimes the emotional encounter with his mother.
We see that* ROSENCRANTZ *and* GUILDENSTERN *have entered the
barn and are joining the audience.*
　　*The mime scene continues until 'Hamlet' stabs 'Polonius' through
the curtain.*
　　The audience of SERVANTS *is loudly appreciative.*

41

The rehearsal continues with a version of the sea journey which is still to come in the plot of Hamlet. The 'boat' is 'performed' by three TRAGEDIANS, ALFRED *taking the part of the female figurehead. A storm blows up and 'Hamlet' leaves the boat, diving into the waves which are 'performed' by three* TRAGEDIANS. *The boat itself disintegrates into the figures of two* TRAGEDIANS *who look around in vain for 'Hamlet'.*

These two TRAGEDIANS *are dressed superficially like* ROSENCRANTZ *and* GUILDENSTERN.

The rehearsal continues with 'Ophelia's' 'mad scene' from Shakespeare's play. Alfred re-enacts the scene giving wild flowers to both 'Claudius' and 'Gertrude'. The rehearsal continues with an impressionistic scene showing 'Ophelia' drowning. She 'drowns' behind a translucent blue cloth.

The rehearsal continues with the scene of 'Ophelia's' burial. 'Hamlet' is in the churchyard, contemplating Yorick's skull. 'Hamlet' sees the dead 'Ophelia' and grapples with 'Laertes'.

The rehearsal continues with the 'duel scene' from Shakespeare's play. 'Hamlet' and 'Laertes' mime the sword fight using imaginary swords. But the sound of the swords clashing is made by an 'offstage' TRAGEDIAN *brandishing two swords together.*

The scene follows the pattern of the Shakespeare scene. 'Hamlet' scores the first point and is offered a drink by 'Claudius'. We have seen 'Claudius' miming the act of putting poison in the goblet. 'Hamlet' declines the drink. 'Gertrude' takes the goblet and toasts 'Hamlet'. 'Claudius' attempts to stop her drinking. But 'Gertrude' drinks from the goblet. 'Claudius' whispers to 'Laertes' and 'Laertes' lunges at 'Hamlet', wounding him. The two duellists fight in earnest. 'Hamlet' disarms 'Laertes' and takes up 'Laertes's' sword. He hands 'Laertes' his own sword. They continue to fight until 'Hamlet', fatally wounded by the poisoned sword, wounds 'Laertes'. By this time 'Gertrude' is on the point of collapse. She falls. 'Laertes' accuses the 'King'. 'Hamlet' kills 'Claudius'. The action resolves itself into the tableau of corpses with which Shakespeare's play ends.

The audience of SERVANTS *applauds mightily.*

PLAYER: Are you familiar with this play?

GUILDENSTERN: No.

(*The* PLAYER *jumps down to join them.*)

PLAYER: A slaughterhouse, eight corpses all told.

GUILDENSTERN: Six.
PLAYER: Eight.

TWO TRAGEDIANS
Dressed superficially as ROSENCRANTZ *and* GUILDENSTERN *dangle broken-necked . . . hanged men. But there are no ropes. They 'hang' on tiptoe.*
GUILDENSTERN: What happened to them?
PLAYER: They are dead.
  (*The audience of* SERVANTS, *etc., have stared at this, absorbed. Now they seem to get the joke all of a sudden and together. They rock with raucous laughter.*)

INT. WINE CELLAR
The PLAYER *strides ahead of . . .* GUILDENSTERN *and* ROSENCRANTZ, *following.*
  GUILDENSTERN *is furious. He is shouting at the back of the retreating* PLAYER.
GUILDENSTERN: Actors! What do you know about death? The mechanics of cheap melodrama!
ROSENCRANTZ: Cheap melodrama!
GUILDENSTERN: It doesn't bring death home to anyone!
ROSENCRANTZ: It's not at home to anyone!
GUILDENSTERN: (*To* ROSENCRANTZ) Shut up!
ROSENCRANTZ: (*To* PLAYER) Shut up!

STAIRCASE
ROSENCRANTZ *and* GUILDENSTERN *run after the* PLAYER, *following him up the stairs.*
GUILDENSTERN: (*Shouts*) You can't do death!
PLAYER: On the contrary, it's what we do best. We have to exploit whatever talent is given to us and our talent is for dying.
  (*The* PLAYER *disappears round the corner at the top of the stairs but his voice continues.*)
We can die heroically, comically, ironically, slowly, suddenly, disgustingly, charmingly . . .
  (ROSENCRANTZ *and* GUILDENSTERN *arrive at a gallery at the top of the stairs. They can hear the* PLAYER's *voice but the* PLAYER *seems to have disappeared. Then they see that he is*

*several feet below them, having evidently leapt over the side of
the gallery.*)
. . . or from a great height!
(*The* PLAYER *crosses the chamber below them, heading for the
furthest door.*)
Audiences know what to expect, and that is all they are
prepared to believe in.
(*The* PLAYER *leaves.*
On the gallery ROSENCRANTZ *and* GUILDENSTERN *relapse.*
ROSENCRANTZ *cups his hands and shouts to the doorway
behind* GUILDENSTERN.)
ROSENCRANTZ: Next!
(GUILDENSTERN *gives him a look. But –*
Suddenly CLAUDIUS *and most of the court surge into view,
walking rapidly.* ROSENCRANTZ *and* GUILDENSTERN *are
caught up in this progress.* CLAUDIUS *takes* GUILDENSTERN *by
the elbow and speaks to him.*)
CLAUDIUS: And can you by no drift of conference
     Get from him why he puts on this confusion?
ROSENCRANTZ: He does confess he feels himself distracted,
     But from what cause a will by no means speak.

INT. CHAPEL, DAY
HAMLET, *in grief, is standing by a tomb which may be presumed to
be the tomb of his father. His lips move. He is mouthing the words
'To be or not to be' but he is inaudible until the next sentence.*
HAMLET: . . . that is the question . . .
     (*He is being spied upon by* CLAUDIUS, GERTRUDE,
     POLONIUS, ROSENCRANTZ *and* GUILDENSTERN. *The
     conversation is in murmurs.*)
GERTRUDE: Did he receive you well?
ROSENCRANTZ: Most like a gentleman.
GUILDENSTERN: But with much forcing of his disposition.
ROSENCRANTZ: Niggard of question, but of our demands
     Most free in his reply.
     (*This is a lie, and* ROSENCRANTZ *and* GUILDENSTERN *know
     it is a lie. Their exchange of glances.*)
GERTRUDE: Did you assay him
     To any pastime?

44

ROSENCRANTZ: Madam, it so fell out that certain players
   We o'erraught on the way. Of these we told him,
   And there did seem in him a kind of joy
   To hear of it. They are here about the court,
   This night to play before him.
POLONIUS: 'Tis most true,
   And he beseech'd me to entreat your Majesties
   To hear and see the matter.
CLAUDIUS: With all my heart; and it doth much content me
   To hear him so inclin'd.
   Good gentlemen, give him a further edge,
   And drive his purpose into these delights.
GUILDENSTERN: We shall, my lord.
   (ROSENCRANTZ *and* GUILDENSTERN *retire.*)
CLAUDIUS: Sweet Gertrude, leave us too,
   For we have closely sent for Hamlet hither,
   That he, as 'twere by accident, may here
   Affront Ophelia.
   (POLONIUS *brings* OPHELIA *forward and places a prayer book
   in her hands.*)

INT. CHAPEL
ROSENCRANTZ *is lying on the flat top of a stone tomb.*
GUILDENSTERN *is exploring nearby.*
ROSENCRANTZ: Do you ever think of yourself as actually dead
   lying in a box with a lid on it?
GUILDENSTERN: No.
ROSENCRANTZ: Nor do I really . . . It's silly to be depressed by
   it. I mean, one thinks of it like being *alive* in a box, one
   keeps forgetting to take into account the fact that one is *dead*
   . . . which should make all the difference . . . shouldn't it? I
   mean, you'd never *know* you were in a box, would you? It
   would be just like you were *asleep* in a box. Not that I'd like
   to sleep in a box, mind you, not without any air – you'd
   wake up dead for a start, and then where would you be? In a
   box. That's the bit I don't like frankly. That's why I don't
   think of it.
      Because you'd be helpless, wouldn't you? Stuffed in a box
   like that, I mean, you'd be in there for ever. Even taking

into account the fact that you're dead, it isn't a pleasant thought. *Especially* if you're dead, really . . . ask yourself, if I asked you straight off – I'm going to stuff you in this box now, would you rather be alive or dead? Naturally you'd prefer to be alive. Life in a box is better than no life at all. I expect. You'd have a chance at least. You could lie there thinking – well, at least I'm not dead! In a minute somebody is going to bang on the lid and tell me to come out.
(*He bangs the tomb with his fist.*)
'Hey, you! What's yer name! Come out of there!'
(*During this* GUILDENSTERN *has been contemplating* ROSENCRANTZ *from close range. He sighs.*)
GUILDENSTERN: I think I'm going to kill you.
(*Loose leaves of printed paper are floating down from above. Two or three fall on* ROSENCRANTZ. *He sits up and, as* GUILDENSTERN *wanders off,* ROSENCRANTZ *starts to make a paper dart. When he has made it, he launches it and lies down again on the tomb.*)
ROSENCRANTZ: I wouldn't think about it, if I were you. You'd only get depressed.

INT. CHAPEL
OPHELIA *is at her prayers.* HAMLET *approaches her and kneels down next to her.*
HAMLET: Nymph, in thy orisons
    Be all my sins remember'd.
OPHELIA: Good, my lord.
    How does your honour for this many a day?
HAMLET: I humbly thank you; well, well, well.
    (ROSENCRANTZ's *paper dart floats past* HAMLET *and* OPHELIA *who don't notice it. The dart continues taking us past* CLAUDIUS *and* POLONIUS *who are spying on* HAMLET. *The dart finally returns to* ROSENCRANTZ. ROSENCRANTZ *plucks the dart out of the air and sits up.*)
ROSENCRANTZ: Whatever became of the moment when one first knew about death? There must have been one, a moment, in childhood, when it first occurred to you that you don't go on for ever. It must have been shattering – stamped into one's

memory. And yet I can't remember it. It never occurred to me at all. We must be born with an intuition of mortality. Before we know the word for it, before we know that there are words, out we come, bloodied and squalling with the knowledge that for all the points of the compass there's only one direction and time is its only measure.

(ROSENCRANTZ *considers his paper dart again. He thinks he might be able to improve it. He starts unfolding it. He starts to fold it differently.*)

GUILDENSTERN
Is walking among the tombs and effigies in the chapel. He begins to hear distant echoing voices. He walks on, following the voices towards a door which has a small hatch in it. GUILDENSTERN *approaches carefully and slides the hatch open. He is shocked by the sight of a masked face in the aperture.*

We see it on the other side of this door, a TRAGEDIAN *is adjusting his mask in a small mirror on his own side of the door.*

GUILDENSTERN *slams the hatch shut and then begins to open it again cautiously.*

ROSENCRANTZ *arrives with his latest paper aeroplane. He has invented the bi-plane. He taps* GUILDENSTERN *on the shoulder, pleased with his invention.* GUILDENSTERN, *concentrating on the hatch, angrily turns round and crumples up the paper plane and stalks away.*

INT. PAINTED HALL, DAY
The TRAGEDIANS, *costumed and masked, have made a stage at one end of the Painted Hall and are in the middle of a dress rehearsal of* The Murder of Gonzago. *The* PLAYER, *without a mask, is not yet in the scene. He is watching the rehearsal from a chair in the body of the empty hall. Behind him,* ROSENCRANTZ *and* GUILDENSTERN *enter cautiously.*

On stage, a King and Queen are in an orchard. The movements are like dance, exaggerated like mime. The 'King' is lying on the grass now, his head in the 'Queen's' lap. She soothes him until he sleeps and she leaves him.

GUILDENSTERN: What is the dumb show for?
PLAYER: It's a device, really – it makes the action that follows

more or less comprehensible. You understand, we are tied down to a language which makes up in obscurity what it lacks in style.

GUILDENSTERN: Is this *The Murder of Gonzago*?

PLAYER: That's the least of it.

ON STAGE

The 'King' sleeps, the 'Poisoner' enters. Very sinister and dramatic. The 'Poisoner' is dressed, superficially, as Claudius. He takes off the sleeper's crown, kisses it. He mimes – pouring poison into the sleeper's ear. The 'Poisoner' leaves. The 'King' convulses, dying . . .

ROSENCRANTZ: Who was that?

PLAYER: The King's brother and uncle to the Prince.

GUILDENSTERN: Not exactly fraternal.

PLAYER: Not exactly avuncular as time goes on.

THE STAGE

The 'Queen' returns, finding the 'King' dead and is full of grief. The 'Poisoner' returns and consoles her. The 'Poisoner' woos the 'Queen' with gifts. She rejects him at first but succumbs, and as the 'Poisoner' embraces her –

OPHELIA

Flings herself on to the stage, through the door at the back, followed by HAMLET *who catches up with her, hysterical, shouting at her.*

HAMLET: Go to, I'll no more on't, it hath made me mad!

(OPHELIA *falls on her knees, weeping.*)

I say we will have no more marriage!

(*The 'Queen' and 'Poisoner' have leapt to their feet and are standing by, appalled and respectful.* HAMLET *notices them.*

He approaches the 'Queen' and 'Poisoner'.)

Those that are married already – all but one – shall live. The rest shall keep as they are.

(*Violently, to* OPHELIA) To a nunnery, go.

(HAMLET *leaps off the stage and leaves through the auditorium, going by . . .*)

ROSENCRANTZ AND GUILDENSTERN

Stand rooted, amazed.

ROSENCRANTZ: That didn't look like love to me.

CLAUDIUS: Love! –
    (*They look at the stage.*)

CLAUDIUS
Is in the act of entering the stage through the same door . . .
POLONIUS *following closely.*
CLAUDIUS: His affections do not that way tend,
      Nor what he spake, though it lack'd form a little,
      Was not like madness.
    (POLONIUS *helps* OPHELIA *to her feet. The* TRAGEDIANS, *who
    have been caught in mid-performance, have backed away,
    wary, respectful.*

      The three of them – CLAUDIUS, POLONIUS, OPHELIA *–
    continue their passage, off the stage, through the auditorium,
    ignoring* ROSENCRANTZ *and* GUILDENSTERN *as they pass
    through the auditorium and out . . .*)
                          There's something in his soul
      O'er which his melancholy sits on brood,
      And I do doubt the hatch and the disclose
      Will be some danger; which for to prevent,
      I have in quick determination
      Thus set it down: he shall with speed to England . . .
    (*This takes the three of them out through the door at the far end
    of the Painted Hall.*)

THE PLAYER
Jumps on to the stage, clapping his hands.
PLAYER: Gentlemen! It doesn't seem to be coming. We are not
    getting it at all. (*To* ROSENCRANTZ *and* GUILDENSTERN)
    What do you think?
GUILDENSTERN: What was I supposed to think?
ROSENCRANTZ: Wasn't that the end?
PLAYER: Do you call that an ending? – with practically everyone
    on his feet? My goodness no – over your dead body. There's
    a design at work in all art – surely you know that? Events
    must play themselves out to an aesthetic, moral and logical
    conclusion.
GUILDENSTERN: And what's that in this case?
PLAYER: It never varies – we aim at the point where everyone
    who is marked for death dies.

GUILDENSTERN: Marked?

PLAYER: Generally speaking, things have gone about as far as
    they can possibly go when things have got about as bad as
    they can reasonably get.

GUILDENSTERN: Who decides?

PLAYER: Decides? It is written. We're tragedians, you see. We
    follow directions – there is no choice involved. The bad end
    unhappily, the good unluckily. That is what tragedy means.
    Next!
    (*From here, the changes of scene taking place on this little stage
    become less and less realistic; that is less and less what would be
    possible in real time.*
        *The orchard has gone. In its place is a miniature of the
    Painted Hall.*)

THE STAGE

The 'Poisoner' and the 'Queen' enter from either side.

PLAYER: Having murdered his brother and wooed the widow,
    the Poisoner mounts the throne! Here we see him and his
    Queen give rein to their unbridled passion!
    (*The 'Poisoner' and the 'Queen' act their 'passion'.*)
    Enter Lucianus, nephew to the king!

THE PLAYER

Is on the stage, alone. He mimes like the rest of the TRAGEDIANS *but
adds a commentary for the benefit of* ROSENCRANTZ *and*
GUILDENSTERN.

PLAYER: Usurped by his uncle and shattered by his mother's
    incestuous marriage . . . He loses his reason . . .
    (*Now the* PLAYER *has a book in his hand, parodying* Hamlet
    . . . A TRAGEDIAN *'Polonius' has joined him . . . The*
    PLAYER *capers and slams the book shut in 'Polonius's' face.*
        The PLAYER *clucks like a chicken.*)
    Throwing the court into turmoil and disarray he alternates
    between bitter melancholy and unrestricted lunacy . . .
    staggering from the suicidal to the merely idle, he has a plan
    to catch the conscience of the King.
    (*He has a cup-and-ball like* Hamlet's. *The ball detonates a
    small bomb of red smoke in the hollow of the cup.*
        Through the smoke as it clears appears a puppet theatre.)

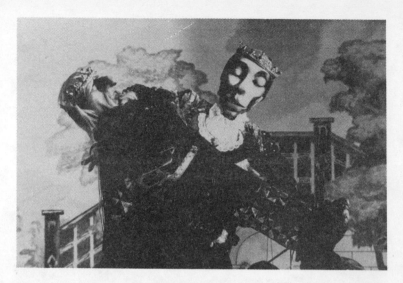

THE PUPPET THEATRE
*Is decked out like the orchard. A puppet King and a puppet Queen
. . . She soothes him and he sleeps . . . a puppet Poisoner enters and
poisons the puppet King. The* TRAGEDIANS *are the 'court', watching
the puppet show.*

The TRAGEDIAN *'Poisoner' interrupts the puppet performance – he
rises from his seat in fear.*

INT. PAINTED HALL, NIGHT
This is a jump cut to the same place at a different time.

The cut is to CLAUDIUS *rising from his chair in fear.*

OPHELIA: The King rises!

HAMLET: What, frighted with false fire?

GERTRUDE: How fares my lord?

POLONIUS: Give o'er the play.

CLAUDIUS: Give me some light. Away.

(*This is the situation.*

We have cut from the dress rehearsal to the same point in The
Murder of Gonzago, *as performed for the Elsinore court.*

*The body of the hall has now been filled with chairs and
couches. The play has been in mid-performance, with an
audience of courtiers. The play has offended the King. The
King,* CLAUDIUS, *is storming out, followed by* GERTRUDE *and*
OPHELIA *and the rest of the court . . . the whole tribe of people
in panic . . . chairs being knocked over in the general turmoil.*

ROSENCRANTZ *and* GUILDENSTERN *have been among this
grand audience.*

ROSENCRANTZ *and* GUILDENSTERN *are attempting to
follow the general exodus, clambering over upturned furniture.*)

ROSENCRANTZ: It wasn't *that* bad . .

(GUILDENSTERN *looks back towards the stage.*)

THE PLAYERS
Are hastily packing up everything.

INT. STAIRCASE
ROSENCRANTZ *and* GUILDENSTERN *walk up the stairs from the
Painted Hall, just as they did when they first entered Elsinore.*

ROSENCRANTZ: There's something they're not telling us.

GUILDENSTERN: What?
ROSENCRANTZ: (*Loudly*) There's something they're not
    telling us.

INT. PAINTED HALL
As before, ROSENCRANTZ *and* GUILDENSTERN *find they have
arrived back at the Painted Hall, looking from the upper doorway
which is above the doorway by which they had left the hall.*
    *The furniture is topsy-turvy, in the state created by the turbulent
exit of the court.* HAMLET *is lying on a couch, playing on a small
wooden pipe.* POLONIUS *enters from the far end of the hall and
approaches him.*
POLONIUS: My lord.
        (HAMLET *takes the pipe away from his lips. He points towards
        the painted ceiling.*)
HAMLET: Do you see yonder cloud that's almost in shape of a
        camel?
POLONIUS: By th' mass and 'tis – like a camel indeed.
HAMLET: Methinks it is like a weasel.
POLONIUS: It is backed like a weasel.
HAMLET: Or like a whale?
POLONIUS: Very like a whale.
HAMLET: Then I will come to my mother by and by . . . – I will
        come by and by.
POLONIUS: I will say so.
HAMLET: 'By and by' is easily said.
        (POLONIUS *leaves.*
            HAMLET *notices* ROSENCRANTZ *and* GUILDENSTERN.)
        Leave me, friends.
        (ROSENCRANTZ *and* GUILDENSTERN *bow and back out of the
        door.*)

INT. CORRIDOR, NIGHT
This is a corridor with doors.
    ROSENCRANTZ *and* GUILDENSTERN *hurry along it. As they do
so, a door just in front of them opens and they are joined by*
CLAUDIUS, *who gives* GUILDENSTERN *a letter, and begins to speak
immediately, keeping pace with* ROSENCRANTZ *and*

GUILDENSTERN, *and when he finishes speaking he exits through another door . . . the whole thing taking place without anybody breaking stride.*

CLAUDIUS: I like him not, nor stands it safe with us
      To let his madness range. Therefore prepare you,
      I your commission will forthwith despatch,
      And he to England shall along with you . . .
    (This is when CLAUDIUS *reaches his exit door, and he disappears through it, and* ROSENCRANTZ *and* GUILDENSTERN *continue on their way.)*

CORRIDOR, NIGHT
ROSENCRANTZ *and* GUILDENSTERN *are still moving at the same pace.*
   They are alone. They can hear voices. They cautiously enter a door in the corridor.

ANTE-CHAMBER
The voices they hear belong to HAMLET *and* GERTRUDE, *who are invisible behind a tapestry on the wall of the room beyond the ante-chamber. They see that* POLONIUS *is listening intently to the unseen conversation.* ROSENCRANTZ *and* GUILDENSTERN *join* POLONIUS *and also listen.* POLONIUS *is not aware of them.* GUILDENSTERN *decides it is time to leave. He taps* ROSENCRANTZ *on the shoulder.* ROSENCRANTZ *nods and taps* POLONIUS *on the shoulder.* POLONIUS *turns round and sees them and panics.*
POLONIUS: What ho! Help, help, help!

GERTRUDE'S BEDROOM
Hearing POLONIUS's *voice,* HAMLET, *who is in the room with* GERTRUDE, *draws his sword and plunges it through the tapestry.*
HAMLET: How now? A rat! Dead for a ducat, dead!
    (On the other side of the tapestry POLONIUS *collapses to the floor.)*
POLONIUS: Oh, I am slain!
    *(*ROSENCRANTZ *and* GUILDENSTERN *are stunned by this turn of events.)*
GERTRUDE: O me, what hast thou done?
HAMLET: Nay, I know not.
      Is it the King?

(HAMLET *raises the tapestry. He looks down on* POLONIUS's *body. He cannot see* ROSENCRANTZ *and* GUILDENSTERN *who have flattened themselves against the wall on either side.* GERTRUDE *is now behind* HAMLET.)

GERTRUDE: O what a rash and bloody deed is this!

HAMLET: A bloody deed. Almost as bad, good mother,
As kill a king and marry with his brother.

GERTRUDE: As kill a king?

HAMLET: Ay, lady, it was my word. –
(*To* POLONIUS's *corpse*)
Thou wretched, rash, intruding fool, farewell.
(*So saying,* HAMLET *lets the tapestry fall back into place and the scene is blacked out.*)

THE SCREEN
Continues black. There is a bump.

GUILDENSTERN'S VOICE: Is that you?

ROSENCRANTZ'S VOICE: I don't know.

GUILDENSTERN'S VOICE: It's you.

ROSENCRANTZ'S VOICE: We're not dead yet, then.
(*There is the sound of a match scraping. The light flares.* ROSENCRANTZ *is holding the match. By now we can hear various sounds which tell us we are at sea on a boat.* ROSENCRANTZ *listens intently.*)
We're on a boat.

GUILDENSTERN: I know.

EXT. THE BOAT DECK, NIGHT
ROSENCRANTZ *and* GUILDENSTERN *come up from below. They are alone.*

ROSENCRANTZ: Dark, isn't it?

GUILDENSTERN: Not for night.

ROSENCRANTZ: No, not for night.

GUILDENSTERN: Dark for day.

ROSENCRANTZ: Oh yes, it's dark for day. Do you think death could possibly be a boat?

GUILDENSTERN: No, no, no . . . death is . . . not. Death isn't. You take my meaning. Death is the ultimate negative. Not-being. You can't not-be on a boat.

54

ROSENCRANTZ: I've frequently not been on boats.

GUILDENSTERN: No, no, no – what you've been is not on boats.

ROSENCRANTZ: I wish I was dead. I could jump over the side. That would put a spoke in their wheel.

GUILDENSTERN: Unless they're counting on it.

ROSENCRANTZ: I shall remain on board. That will put a spoke in their wheel.

(*So saying, he trips and falls down a hatch.*)

INT. BOAT, NIGHT

GUILDENSTERN *comes down a ladder from the deck. There is no sign of* ROSENCRANTZ. *He has fallen straight through a second hatch, into the bowels of the boat.* GUILDENSTERN *peers into the hatch.*

GUILDENSTERN: Are you all right?

ROSENCRANTZ: (*His voice echoing*) Yes. Why?

GUILDENSTERN: Would you like to come up now?

ROSENCRANTZ: All right. Thank you.

(ROSENCRANTZ *emerges from the hatch.* GUILDENSTERN *helps him up.*)

Nice bit of planking, that.

GUILDENSTERN: Yes.

ROSENCRANTZ: Beautiful bilges.

GUILDENSTERN: Yes.

ROSENCRANTZ: Lovely bottom on her.

GUILDENSTERN: (*Impatiently*) Yes, I'm very fond of boats myself.

(ROSENCRANTZ *and* GUILDENSTERN *are in a space between decks.*)

I like the way they're contained. You don't have to worry about which way to go, or whether to go at all – the question doesn't arise, because you're on a *boat* aren't you? . . . I think I'll spend most of my life on boats.

ROSENCRANTZ: Very healthy.

GUILDENSTERN: One is free on a boat. For a time. Relatively.

ROSENCRANTZ: I think I'm going to be sick.

(ROSENCRANTZ *blunders away among ropes and bollards.*)

THROUGH A WINDOW

A lighted cabin: HAMLET's *asleep.*

   ROSENCRANTZ's *face at the window, looking in.*

   ROSENCRANTZ *hurries back to join* GUILDENSTERN.

ROSENCRANTZ: He's there!

GUILDENSTERN: What's he doing?

ROSENCRANTZ: Sleeping.

GUILDENSTERN: It's all right for him.

ROSENCRANTZ: What is?

GUILDENSTERN: He can sleep.

ROSENCRANTZ: It's all right for him.

GUILDENSTERN: He's got us now.

ROSENCRANTZ: He can sleep.

GUILDENSTERN: It's all done for him.

ROSENCRANTZ: He's got us.

GUILDENSTERN: And we've got nothing . . .

ROSENCRANTZ: And we've got nothing.

GUILDENSTERN: (*Turning on him furiously*) Why don't you say something original! You don't take me up on anything – you just repeat it in a different order.

ROSENCRANTZ: I can't think of anything original. I'm only good in support.

GUILDENSTERN: I'm sick of making the running.

ROSENCRANTZ: Oh, what's going to become of us!

   (*He starts sniffing back tears.* GUILDENSTERN *repents and comforts him.*)

GUILDENSTERN: It's all right . . . there, there. I'll see we're all right.

ROSENCRANTZ: But we've got nothing to go on. We're out on our own.

GUILDENSTERN: We're on our way to England. We're taking Hamlet to the English King.

ROSENCRANTZ: What for?

GUILDENSTERN: What for? Where have you been?

ROSENCRANTZ: When?

GUILDENSTERN: We've got a letter. You remember the letter.

ROSENCRANTZ: Do I?

GUILDENSTERN: Everything is explained in the letter.

ROSENCRANTZ: Is that it, then?

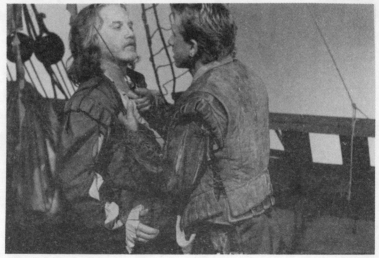

GUILDENSTERN: What?

ROSENCRANTZ: We take Hamlet to the English King, we hand over the letter – what then?

GUILDENSTERN: That's it – we're finished.

ROSENCRANTZ: Who is the English King?

GUILDENSTERN: That depends on when we get there.

ROSENCRANTZ: So we've got a letter which explains everything?

GUILDENSTERN: You've got it.

ROSENCRANTZ: I thought you had it.

GUILDENSTERN: I do have it.

ROSENCRANTZ: You have it?

GUILDENSTERN: You've got it.

ROSENCRANTZ: I don't get it.

GUILDENSTERN: You haven't got it.

ROSENCRANTZ: I just said that.

GUILDENSTERN: I've got it.

ROSENCRANTZ: (*Understanding*) Oh, I've got it.

GUILDENSTERN: Shut up.

ROSENCRANTZ: Right. What a shambles! We're just not getting anywhere. Not even England. I don't believe in it anyway.

GUILDENSTERN: Just a conspiracy of cartographers, you mean?

ROSENCRANTZ: And even if it's true, the King of England won't know what we're talking about. What are we going to say?

GUILDENSTERN: We say – Your Majesty, we have arrived!

(ROSENCRANTZ *takes on a regal personality*.)

ROSENCRANTZ: And who are you?

GUILDENSTERN: We are Rosencrantz and Guildenstern.

ROSENCRANTZ: Never heard of you!

GUILDENSTERN: Well, we're nobody special –

ROSENCRANTZ: What's your game?

GUILDENSTERN: We've got our instructions –

ROSENCRANTZ: First I've heard of it.

GUILDENSTERN: Let me finish! We've come from Denmark.

ROSENCRANTZ: What do you want?

GUILDENSTERN: Nothing – we're delivering Hamlet –

ROSENCRANTZ: Who's he?

GUILDENSTERN: You've heard of *him* –

ROSENCRANTZ: Oh I've heard of him all right and I want nothing to do with it.

GUILDENSTERN: But –

ROSENCRANTZ: You march in here without so much as a by-your-leave and expect me to take in every lunatic you try to pass off with a lot of unsubstantiated –

GUILDENSTERN: (*Producing it and flourishing it*) We've got a letter!

(ROSENCRANTZ *tears the letter open.*)

ROSENCRANTZ: I see . . . I see . . . Well, this seems to support your story such as it is – it is an exact command from the King of Denmark for several different reasons, importing Denmark's health and England's too, that on the reading of this letter, without delay, I should have Hamlet's head cut off – !

(GUILDENSTERN *snatches the letter and looks at it.*
   They look at each other, aghast.)

HAMLET
Is eavesdropping on them. He quietly closes the door of his cabin.

ROSENCRANTZ AND GUILDENSTERN
Come to the window of his cabin. They watch HAMLET, *who is lying on his bunk with his eyes closed. When they move away from the window* HAMLET *opens his eyes.*

INT. ROSENCRANTZ'S AND GUILDENSTERN'S CABIN, NIGHT
There is some light from a candle. GUILDENSTERN *is also using the candle to soften the broken seal on the letter. When the wax is soft,* GUILDENSTERN *presses a coin on to it to fake a seal. During this –*

ROSENCRANTZ: We're his *friends.*

GUILDENSTERN: How do you know?

ROSENCRANTZ: From our young days brought up with him.

GUILDENSTERN: You've only got their word for it.

ROSENCRANTZ: But that's what we depend on.

GUILDENSTERN: Well, yes, and then again no. Let us keep things in proportion. Assume, if you like, that they're going to kill him. Well, he is a man, he is mortal, death comes to us all, etc., and consequently he would have died anyway, sooner or later. And then again, what is so terrible about death? As Socrates so philosophically put it, since we don't know what death is, it is illogical to fear it. It might be . . .

very nice. Or to look at it another way, we are little men, we don't know the ins and outs of the matter, there are wheels within wheels, etc. – All in all, I think we'd be well advised to leave well alone.

(GUILDENSTERN *finishes the job to his satisfaction.*)

ROSENCRANTZ: It's awful.

GUILDENSTERN: But it could have been worse. I was beginning to think it was.

(GUILDENSTERN *lies down on his bunk. He puts his hands behind his head, crosses his legs, smiles, and looks quite pleased with the world.*

ROSENCRANTZ *prepares for sleep. For this he uses earplugs and a sleeping mask.* GUILDENSTERN *watches him.*)

ROSENCRANTZ: Good night!

(ROSENCRANTZ *blows at the candle but because he has a sleeping mask on he misses. He lies down and goes to sleep.*)

INT. HAMLET'S CABIN, NIGHT
HAMLET *is writing a letter. His quill scratches busily over the parchment lit by his lantern.*

INT. ROSENCRANTZ'S AND GUILDENSTERN'S CABIN, NIGHT
ROSENCRANTZ *and* GUILDENSTERN *are asleep.* HAMLET *enters with a letter he has been writing. He changes over the two letters. As he is leaving the cabin he hears, faintly at first, the beginning of a sea battle, the boom of a cannon . . .*

INT. ROSENCRANTZ'S AND GUILDENSTERN'S CABIN, NIGHT
A cannon ball rips through one wall of the cabin and takes a large chunk out of another wall. GUILDENSTERN *sits up.* ROSENCRANTZ *continues to sleep.* GUILDENSTERN *reaches for his sword and clambers through the large hole in the wall. There is now a considerable din all around.*

GUILDENSTERN
Finds himself in a space between decks. He looks around for escape. He looks up. The space is roofed with a canvas sheet which bulges and heaves with unseen bodies. But then a cutlass rips through the ceiling and slits it open. An immense cascade falls down into the

interior of the boat. There are several people and a ton of stuff descending in the cascade. The TRAGEDIANS *and all of their possessions are falling through the ceiling. The noise of battle continues.*

Finally the PLAYER *struggles free from the pile.*

PLAYER: All in the same boat then. What do you make of it so far?

GUILDENSTERN: What's happening?

PLAYER: Pirates!

(*The other* TRAGEDIANS *are surfacing from the pile.*)

(*Shouts*) Everyone on stage!

(*The roof is now open to the sounds and sights of the bombardment.*)

INT. ROSENCRANTZ'S AND GUILDENSTERN'S CABIN

ROSENCRANTZ *is still asleep.*

The din has been continuous.

A CANNON BALL

Rips through the wooden partition above his body.

ROSENCRANTZ *sits bolt upright (he still has his sleeping mask over his eyes) – just in time to avoid being speared by a cutlass which bursts through the partition next to his pillow and is then withdrawn.* ROSENCRANTZ *lies back down again, knowing nothing.*

With a splintering roar, the painted bowsprit of another boat crashes into the cabin.

The bowsprit takes the form of a carved woman naked to the waist. Nicely painted. She comes to rest over ROSENCRANTZ, *who removes his sleeping mask. He is finally waking up, slightly puzzled by the naked woman staring into his face.*

Then the two boats part company. The figurehead of the invading boat leaves the cabin by the way she came.

ROSENCRANTZ *sits up, definitely alert.*

He looks through the hole in the side of his own boat and sees HAMLET, *swinging on a rope, land on the prow of the departing boat.*

ROSENCRANTZ *removes his earplugs, catching up on the situation, and appalled.*

ROSENCRANTZ: Hamlet!

INT. BOAT DECK, DAWN

ROSENCRANTZ *and* GUILDENSTERN *emerge on deck through a hatch. They are alone.*

GUILDENSTERN: Where's Hamlet?

ROSENCRANTZ: Gone.

GUILDENSTERN: Gone where?

ROSENCRANTZ: The pirates took him.

GUILDENSTERN: But he can't – we're supposed to be – we've got a *letter* – which says – the whole thing's pointless without him – we need Hamlet for our release!

(ROSENCRANTZ *has an idea.*)

ROSENCRANTZ: I'll pretend to be him –

(*Then he has a better idea.*)

You pretend to be him –

(*He abandons both ideas.*)

We'll be all right. I suppose we just go on.

GUILDENSTERN: Go where?

ROSENCRANTZ: To England.

GUILDENSTERN: England! – I don't believe it!

ROSENCRANTZ: Just a conspiracy of cartographers, you mean.

GUILDENSTERN: I don't believe any of it! And what do we say?

ROSENCRANTZ: We say – We've arrived!

THE PLAYER

Approaches out of the smoke. He wears 'costume' as an English King.

PLAYER: And who are you?

ROSENCRANTZ: We are Guildenstern and Rosencrantz.

PLAYER: Which is which?

ROSENCRANTZ: Well, I'm Guildenstern –

GUILDENSTERN: And he's Rosencrantz.

ROSENCRANTZ: Exactly.

PLAYER: I don't begin to understand.

GUILDENSTERN: (*Producing the letter*) We have a letter!

PLAYER: A letter!

(*He takes it and opens it, and reads it.*)

'As England is Denmark's faithful tributary . . . as love between them like the palm might flourish, etc. . . . that on the knowing of this contents, without delay of any kind . . .

should those bearers, Rosencrantz and Guildenstern, put to sudden death.'

ROSENCRANTZ: Not that letter. (*To* GUILDENSTERN) Give him the other one.

GUILDENSTERN: I haven't got another one.

(*The* PLAYER *takes off his crown and his cloak, and resumes his own personality.*)

PLAYER: They've gone! It's all over!

THE TRAGEDIANS

Converge. They come through hatches. They come down ropes. They pop out of casks . . .

GUILDENSTERN: (*Quietly*) Where we went wrong was getting on a boat. We can move, of course, change direction, rattle about, but our movement is contained within a larger one that carries us idly towards eternity without possibility of reprieve or hope of explanation.

ROSENCRANTZ: They had it in for us, didn't they? Right from the beginning. Who'd have thought that we were so important?

GUILDENSTERN: But why? Was it all for this? Who are we that so much should converge on our little deaths? Who are we?

PLAYER: You are Rosencrantz and Guildenstern. That's enough.

GUILDENSTERN: No, it is not enough. To be told so little – to such an end – and still, finally, to be denied an explanation –

PLAYER: In our experience, almost everything ends in death.

GUILDENSTERN: Your experience! Actors!

(*He snatches a dagger from the* PLAYER's *belt and holds it at the* PLAYER's *throat.*)

I'm talking about death and you've never experienced that. You die a thousand casual deaths and then come back in a different hat. But no one gets up after death – there is no applause – there is only silence and some second-hand clothes, and *that's* – death!

(GUILDENSTERN *rams the dagger into the* PLAYER's *body. He leaves it there, plunged in up to the hilt. The* PLAYER *topples backwards through a large hatch in the deck and falls heavily on*

to the deck below. ROSENCRANTZ *and* GUILDENSTERN *come
to the edge of the hatch and look down on the* PLAYER, *who lies
still.*)
If we have a destiny, then so had he – and if this is ours,
then that was his – and if there are no explanations for us,
then let there be none for him.
(*From all sides, the* TRAGEDIANS *approach the* PLAYER'S
body. After a moment they start to applaud. The PLAYER *stands
up, brushing himself down.*)
PLAYER: Oh, come, come, gentlemen – no flattery – it was
   merely competent. (*To* GUILDENSTERN) You see, it is the
   kind you do believe in, it's what is expected.
   (*He demonstrates how the dagger's blade retracts into the hilt.*)
   Deaths for all ages and occasions!

ELSINORE MONTAGE
We see OPHELIA *under water, drowned; and* LAERTES *wounding*
HAMLET; *and* HAMLET *wounding* LAERTES; *and* GERTRUDE
collapsing, the poisoned goblet falling from her hand; and HAMLET,
dying, killing CLAUDIUS *with his sword.*

THE BOAT
The scene is as before.
PLAYER: Deaths of kings and princes . . . and nobodies!
   (*He gestures up towards* ROSENCRANTZ *and* GUILDENSTERN.
      Now the TRAGEDIANS *hastily start packing up their
   possessions, throwing them into (strangely enough) their cart. It
   is as though the cart had been incorporated into the structure of
   the boat. Thus, when the* TRAGEDIANS *hurl some of their
   possessions up on to the roof of the 'cart' and we see that*
   ROSENCRANTZ *and* GUILDENSTERN *are standing up there,
   now with ropes round their necks. It is no longer clear whether
   we are with the cart or with the boat.*)
ROSENCRANTZ: That's it then, is it?
   (*Pause.*)
   We've done nothing wrong. We didn't harm anyone, did
   we?
GUILDENSTERN: I can't remember.
ROSENCRANTZ: All right, then, I don't care. I've had enough.
   To tell you the truth, I'm relieved.

GUILDENSTERN: Our names shouted in a certain dawn . . . a
    message . . . a summons . . . there must have been a
    moment at the beginning, where we could have said no. But
    somehow we missed it. Well, we'll know better next time.
    (GUILDENSTERN *shuts his eyes.*)
PLAYER: Till then.
    (ROSENCRANTZ *shuts his eyes.*)

ELSINORE
A man (the ENGLISH AMBASSADOR*) is walking the length of the
Painted Hall. He arrives at Gertrude's goblet. He picks it up. In
front of him is the tableau of corpses which is the end of
Shakespeare's play.*
AMBASSADOR: The sight is dismal;
    And our affairs from England come too late.
    The ears are senseless that should give us hearing
    To tell him his commandment is fulfill'd,
    That Rosencrantz and Guildenstern are dead.
    (*Against the sky we see the two ropes straighten. We do not see
    the two men hanging from them.*
        The TRAGEDIANS *are folding up the side of the cart . . .
    which now moves away from the camera and is seen to be
    moving away from us through the woods where we first saw it.*)

SKYLINE
In the distance against the sky, the cart, with the TRAGEDIANS
walking with it, continues its journey.